Ellen Sm

Eric Ogden

Acknowledgements

While many people assisted me with the production of this history, two in particular were instrumental in providing both information and illustrations. I am grateful to Betty Smith, wife of the late Eric Smith, the final managing director, for making her photographic collection available to me and for much background information. My grateful thanks also to Douglas Neal, associated with the family company from 1965, who also provided many illustrations and gave me an insight into the driver's part in coach operation. His knowledge of the company and his experiences and anecdotes added much to this book.

My thanks also to Barry Drelincourt, former Operations Director of Rossendale Transport, who put me in touch with Betty Smith; former Ellen Smith employees Ken Barker, Douglas Harper and Alan Schofield; Noel Ogden for typing and computer work; Jonathan Hird for computer assistance; George Turnbull and Paul Wotton of the Greater Manchester Transport Museum; Julian Jefferson, Rochdale Local Studies Officer; Peter Greaves, John Holmes and Harry Postlethwaite. The following publications have been helpful: Leyland Journal, Coach & Bus Week, Coachmart, Route One, Rochdale Observer, PSV Circle.

Illustrations have been credited where the photographers are known and I am grateful to those who have taken photographs especially for this book. Some images bore no details of the photographers on the back and they are credited to the various collections from whence they came. Nevertheless we are grateful for their use to add to the interest of the book.

As always thanks are due to Scott Hellewell, David & Mary Shaw, Colin Reeve and Mark Senior for reading and layout and to John Senior of Venture Publications Ltd for his technical, design and publishing skills.

Eric Ogden 16 June 2009

LUXURY TRAVEL
LEYLAND TIGER & LEYLAND LIONESS COACHES
18. 20. 24. 26. 28 & 32 SEATERS

E. SMITH
MOTOR COACH BOOKING STATION
WARDLEWORTH BROW. ROCHDALE

PHONES ROCHDALE 3067
LITTLEBOROUGH 8119

H. J. STEWARD
PHOTOGRAPHER. ROCHDALE

In this 1931 photograph 1930 Burlingham-bodied Leyland LTB1 DK 6440, 1929 Lewis and Crabtree-bodied Leyland LTB1 DK 5819 and new Leyland TS1 DK 7182, also with Burlingham body, line up outside the Wardleworth garage. *(BSC)*

Introduction

Just inside the entrance to Ellen Smith's garage, to the left in the 1984 photograph, can be seen the wooden bench where, on my visits, I would sit with either Harry or Eric Smith and Ken Barker, their chief engineer. We would discuss the coaches, the excursions, the state of the industry and their preference for British-built vehicles. The lean-to office at the left of the garage was the domain of Marjorie Smith, Harry's wife. It was always a pleasure to chat with all three Smiths who were invariably pleased to welcome anyone with an interest in coaches and coaching. It was only recently that I met Betty Smith, Eric's wife, and enjoyed her hospitality. She kindly provided me with information and made her photograph collection available to me for this book.

A much appreciated advantage of travelling with Ellen Smith was the provision of safe car parking at the garage. My regular place was at the left of the above-mentioned picture alongside the office. On returning from London at about midnight it was a boon to have the car available on the spot for the drive back to Saddleworth. Such an excursion would not have been possible otherwise. One of the Smiths was always there to see the coach home. I have happy memories of day trips to London and the NEC at Birmingham for the Motor Show. In later years there was the pleasure of travelling on the Leyland Royal Tiger Doyens, the top-flight British coaches of their day with their outstanding ride, both quiet and smooth.

I recall with pleasure and appreciation the geniality of Harry, Eric and Marjorie and the excursions taken in their coaches.

Wardleworth Garage, Yorkshire Street, Rochdale in 1984. *(EOC)*

Where it all began; Fred Smith's house and booking office in Church Street, Littleborough. The sign above the door states *"E. Smith"* but the rest is indistinct in this early photograph. Harry Smith was an expert signwriter and painted these as well as all the excursion boards outside the garage, the Newgate office and the booking agents in the area. *(DNC)*

Origins

Back in the nineteenth century Ellen Gilson and Lund Smith lived on farms opposite each other high on the moors above Oxenhope, West Yorkshire. They met and fell in love but encountered opposition from their families so much so that they eloped over the Pennine Hills to Littleborough in Lancashire and were married at the parish church there. They continued to farm at Moss Barn Farm. Ellen sold candles and eggs to enable her to pay for lessons in reading and writing, basic skills which were to stand her in good stead and develop her acumen for her future business life which she surely could not have foreseen. Like many long-established coach and bus operators, the origins of Ellen Smith (Tours) Ltd of Rochdale in Lancashire dated back to horse-drawn days at the end of the nineteenth century.

In 1900, as an adjunct to his farming interests, Lund Smith began operating in 1900 a haulage business with horses, and a passenger service between Littleborough and Rochdale with horse-drawn wagonettes. Lund died in 1907 and Ellen continued the business with the help of three of their five sons, Miles, Fred and Percy. Of the other sons, Harry died young, and Lewis was in the Army during the First World War, suffering shell shock to the extent that he was unable to take any part in the business after the war. There were also two daughters, Gertie and Cissie. As the three sons gradually assumed control of the day to day operation, Ellen continued to finance the business. She retained a keen interest in the affairs and often appeared at the garage to ensure that all was well. That all was well was evident by the fact that the business continued successfully until the death or retirement of her grandsons Harry, son of Miles, and Eric, son of Fred. Harry said that Ellen 'ruled with a rod of iron.'

The first motor lorry, a Manchester-built Belsize with solid tyres, registered DK 594, was acquired in 1915. As was common at the time, the lorry body was taken off and replaced with a passenger-carrying body at the weekends and on public and Wakes holidays. A removal van body of tongue and groove timber construction bound with iron strapping, typical of the period, was fitted to this and other chassis as required. This van body, an early form of container, survived at the back of the Wardleworth garage well into the 1980s. It was later donated by Eric Smith to the Greater Manchester Transport Museum at Boyle Street, Manchester where it resides today (2009). The main haulage business was the carrying of cotton bales as Rochdale was within the Lancashire textile industry centred on Manchester.

Removals constituted another part of the Smith business. Other chassis acquired during the 1920s included Daimler, Maudslay and Leyland and an ex-War Department Karrier. The haulage vehicles travelled throughout England until that side of the business was discontinued in the early 1930s. One of the earliest long distance passenger adventures was a holiday tour to London, Brighton and Eastbourne in 1920, travelling in solid-tyred Daimler charabanc TB 2788. The back of a photograph taken on this tour states 'G Stansfield & friend,' the real name of Gracie Fields. It is known that Gracie Fields aged 13 and a school friend were passengers in a similar holiday tour to Torquay in 1911 organised by the Holt family, predecessor of that other well-known Rochdale operator, Yelloway Motor Services Ltd. Gracie's father, Fred, a mill engineer, went along as a driver/mechanic.

It would seem that Gracie was partial to charabanc holiday tours! Like Ellen Smith's directors, Yelloway's Hubert Allen would buy only British vehicles. The Smith tradition of buying only British was continued to the end by Harry and Eric. After three Albions in 1925, 1926 and 1927, almost all subsequent vehicles were Leylands. The first of the Albions, TD 2333, an 18-seater, was an early example of a coach fitted with pneumatic tyres all round at a time when most coaches retained solid tyres on the rear wheels.

A 1920s advertisement showing a box van fitted to a Leyland chassis. This would be replaced with a charabanc body for passenger use at weekends and holiday periods. Note the extreme rear overhang. *(DH)*

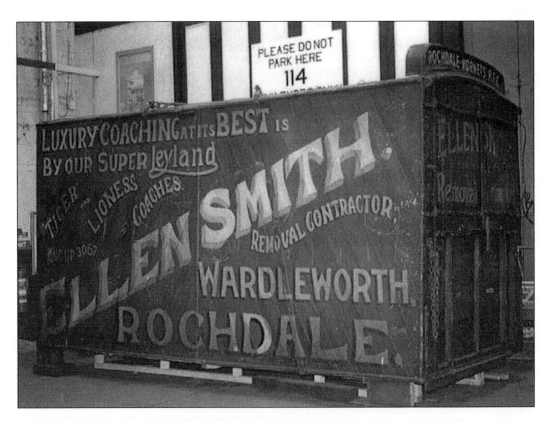

The box van body on its arrival at the Greater Manchester Transport Museum having been donated by Eric Smith as a rare piece of transport history. Note the angled tongue and groove timber sides with iron strappings for lifting in the manner of modern containers, and the elaborate sign writing. *(GMTS)*

Above: FY 4140, a 1921 Leyland M-type charabanc, in Eastbourne, 1923. New in 1921 to Thompson & Culshaw, Southport, it was acquired by Ellen Smith in 1922, later rebodied as a saloon, then sold to Morris of Newton Heath in 1934 and converted to a lorry. Fred Smith, Eric's father, is standing on the left. *(KB)*

Below: TD 2333, a 1925 Albion PF24 with a Burlingham 18-seat charabanc body, DK 4081, a 1927 Leyland Lioness with a J. Crabtree 26-seat body and TD 6328, a 1926 Albion PFA26 20-seat Burlingham dual-doored coach are lined up at Wardleworth garage in 1927. The signwriting on the window at the right offers a long Whitsuntide weekend at Blackpool for a return fare of ten shillings (50p). *(BSC)*

Above: TB 2788, a 1920 Daimler CK charabanc on a holiday tour to London, Brighton and Eastbourne, an ambitious venture for the time in such a vehicle. The back of the original photograph states "G Stansfield & friend." Was this the later entertainer Gracie Fields who was known to have enjoyed charabanc holiday tours?

Below: TB 2788 again, perhaps on a different tour. *(BSC both)*

Charabancs

The first true passenger charabanc was a Leyland M type registered FY 4140 which was new to Thompson and Culshaw of Southport in 1921 and was acquired by the business the following year. Harry Smith told the story about his father Miles driving through Burnley with his horses and wagon. He stopped at the Leyland dealer's showroom to look in the window and spotted the Leyland charabanc.

The salesman, a Mr Tillotson, came out to him and the outcome was that Miles agreed to purchase it. He drove home to obtain the cash from his mother, Ellen, and returned to Burnley the next day with a tin box full of one pound notes! This vehicle was still working as a lorry with Morris of Newton Heath, Manchester in 1935.

Ellen Smith occupied the site in Yorkshire Street, Wardleworth, Rochdale when land was purchased in 1925. The garage was built in the centre of the plot leaving parking space around the building. In the 1970's more land was dug away at the back to allow more parking space, including space for withdrawn vehicles. A lean-to office was attached to the left side of the garage circa 1965 which also served as a booking office. Later, a travel shop was opened at Newgate in the town centre succeeding a booking office there, at first managed by Percy Smith. By 1989 there were booking agents at Oldham, Royton, Shaw, Heywood, Milnrow, Bacup, Rawtenstall and Waterfoot in Lancashire and Hebden Bridge and Todmorden in Yorkshire. Eric Smith looked for agents who were open early and late and on Sundays such as newsagents and off-licences, as well as the more usual travel agents, since there was a wider exposure to potential customers.

All-Leyland fleet

The Leyland fleet standard commenced in earnest in 1927 with bonneted Lionesses following Harry's father's advice to buy only Leylands. The odd AEC, Bedford and Daimler were tried post-war, and two 1962 Bedford SB5s were taken over from Benjamin Barnes & Son of Rawtenstall in 1964 (539/40 XTF). Powered by Leyland engines, they were retained for only three years, and the few other lightweight Bedfords bought new remained in the fleet for a maximum of five years. In contrast, many Leylands gave over 15 years service and some over 20 years. After the Lionesses, Tigers were bought from 1931, the last pre-war vehicle being a TS7 with Harrington 'tail-fin' body in 1936 (ADK 989) which Harry himself drove and which remained in service for 20 years. The first radio-equipped coach was one of the TS4 Tigers in 1932 (DK 7757/8). The striking Leaping Tiger crest applied to the sides of the coaches, first in a triangle then in a circle, appeared in the early 1930s on the Leyland Tigers. It is said that the first hand-painted image was copied from a cigarette card. This skilful freehand painting was carried out by Jack Mills who was trained as a professional painter. The design was used by Leyland as the badge for the Royal Tiger coach from 1949. The same design was used as the sign for the Royal Tiger pub in Leyland.

While only Leyland chassis were purchased from 1927 up to the outbreak of war, bodywork was much more varied. Lioness bodies were by Burlingham of Blackpool and local coachbuilders Lewis & Crabtree and Fielden & Bottomley.

Lewis & Crabtree of Heywood became Shearing & Crabtree of Oldham who bodied two Tigers in 1932 (DK 7757/8), the Shearing being Herbert Shearing of Oldham who was an operator in his own right. Following his retirement after the war the firm bearing his name passed through various ownerships, eventually becoming Shearings Holidays Ltd of Wigan. In the early 1990s, Shearings became Britain's largest coach operator, merging with its great rival Wallace Arnold in 2005. The body of the first Lioness (DK 4081) in 1927 was built at Heywood by Jack Crabtree in one week. Harry Smith told of the high standard of this body, recalling that it never had to return to the builders for rectification. He said that Jack Crabtree was ahead of his time. While most coachbuilders at the time built directly onto the chassis, he had sides, backs and floors already built, ready to be incorporated into the complete vehicle.

The company's printed booklet of 96 pages produced in 1935 described no less than 146 destinations, from Alton Towers to York and three separate routes round the Yorkshire Dales. There were excursions to various destinations in North Wales and five different routes to Blackpool. Post-war, continental tours were not favoured though short shopping trips to the French Channel ports were offered and proved very popular. On private

TD 2333, the 1925 Albion PF24 model with a Burlingham 18-seat body, on a Scottish tour in July 1926. This vehicle later became a lorry in the Manchester area. *(BSC)*

TD 6328, a 1926 Albion PFA26 with a 20-seat Burlingham coach body on a ladies trip to Southport. *(BSC)*

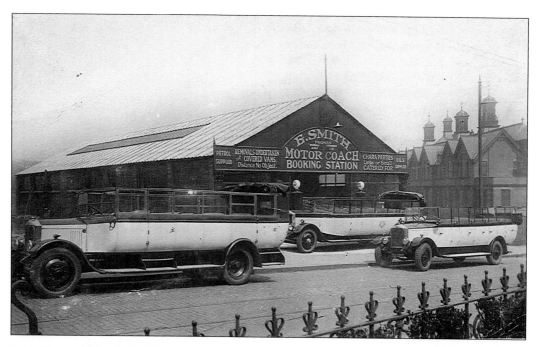

TD 6328, TD 2333 and DK 4081 line up outside the Wardleworth garage. The legal lettering behind the front mudguard on TD 6328 states '2mph'. *(BSC)*

1928 Burlingham-bodied Leyland LTB4 DK 5053 was commandeered by the Ministry of Supply in 1941. It passed to Fairclough of Wigan in 1943 and to Webster of Wigan two years later. *(EOC)*

hire, however, school party and twin town visits were made to the continent, but Marjorie was always reluctant to send coaches abroad. Another speciality was the conveyance of rugby football fans, and Rochdale Hornets Rugby League team was carried over a period of 60 years. The drivers' experience was that the Rugby League teams and their supporters were not much trouble. Far worse were the Rugby Union groups who were not encouraged as coaches were found to require more interior cleaning and repair. It was not unknown for members of these groups to take up the floor panels. Douglas Neal recalled the time around 1975 at Aust services on returning from a Rugby match at Neath when a streaker left the coach and ran round the service area, no doubt for a bet. On his return, Douglas was ready to make a hasty exit. Much work was undertaken for charitable institutions such as senior citizens' clubs and blind societies.

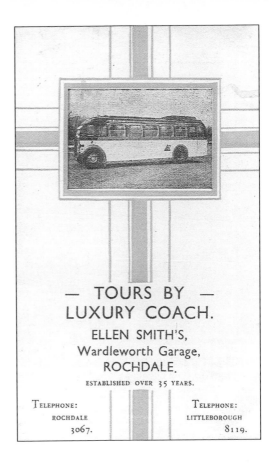

— TOURS BY —
LUXURY COACH.
ELLEN SMITH'S,
Wardleworth Garage,
ROCHDALE.
ESTABLISHED OVER 35 YEARS.

TELEPHONE:
ROCHDALE
3067.

TELEPHONE:
LITTLEBOROUGH
8119.

Watched by two farmers and a dog, DK 9092, a 1934 Burlingham-bodied Leyland TS6, rests at the top of the Kirkstone Pass while on a Lake District excursion.

Above: Three Leyland Tiger coaches line up outside the Wardleworth Garage. DK 8356, a 1933 TS4 model with 32-seat body by Charles Roberts of Horbury near Wakefield, is at the front. Behind are two more TS4s, DK 7758 and DK 7757, both with Harrington bodies. Notice the variation in the Tiger motif. On the first coach the Tiger is leaping out of a triangle. *(BSC)*

Below: An official photograph of DK 8356 when new. Note the hinged extension panel at the front, the Roberts logo behind the front wheel representing railway lines, the hinged steps to reach the roof-mounted luggage rack with its waterproof cover, the sliding roof and the curtains. This was an altogether new concept in coaching compared to charabancs and the canvas-topped Albions and Leyland Lionesses. *(BSC)*

Above: In this second official photograph of DK 8356 the window louvres denote some of the destinations served by Ellen Smith; Chester, Blackpool, Morecambe, Southport and Scarborough on the nearside and London, Bournemouth, Gretna Green, Llandudno and Torquay on the offside – quite a wide coverage of the country. *(BSC)*

Below: This interior view of DK 8356 shows the opening roof, padded luggage racks, curtains, clock, decorative ashtrays and rope pulls on the sumptuous leather and moquette seating. With ornamental lighting and art deco bulkhead it appears to be short only of carpeting. *(BSC)*

DK 8356 was requisitioned by the Ministry of Supply for the War Department from 1940 to 1946. On its return it was rebodied in the garage to a Challenger design based on a pre-war Harrington shape. After being withdrawn in 1956 it saw further service with a Todmorden concern. *(JJH)*

ADK 989 was a Harrington-bodied TS7. The only photograph showing this coach which has come to light shows it parked up with other coaches in Blackpool. The last pre-war coach, it remained in service for 20 years. *(PGC)*

World War 2

On the outbreak of the Second World War in September 1939, all excursions and tours came to an end. Some work was available on behalf of the government, especially the transport of prisoners of war from their accommodation to their daily work in local mills and factories. Italian prisoners were also put to work on building the Kirkholt housing estate in Rochdale and Ellen Smith was also directed to transport them. Consequently, Harry Smith remained with the business throughout the war. During the war Eric Smith served with the Royal Navy, mostly in motor torpedo boats based in Gosport. Jack Mills and Ken Barker, the engineer, also served in the Royal Navy. At least two coaches were commandeered by the War Department and did not return. Others are thought to have been requisitioned and returned. Of the eleven coaches owned in 1939, nine survived in 1945. On joining the company in 1946, Eric Smith obtained his PSV licence. He spent much of his time driving but also carried out administrative and engineering work as required.

Post-war

The first post-war coach was a Leyland PS1/1 Tiger bodied by Plaxton in 1947 (FDK 731). Harrington bodies were then in favour but after that coachbuilder ceased production in 1966, Plaxton became the desired builder for the remainder of the Smiths' involvement in the company. Small exceptions were Burlingham, Duple and Challenger and the final Royal Tiger Doyens which were semi-integral vehicles wholly built by Leyland. After the war, Jack Crabtree built bodies in Oldham under the name of Challenger, two of which went to Ellen Smith in 1948 (GDK 121/2). The design of the Challenger bodies was based on the pre-war Harrington.

Apparently the pre-war quality did not carry over into post-war years since the two 1948 Tigers were re-bodied by Burlingham in 1955 after which both vehicles went on to serve for another nine years.

The post-war fleet continued with Leylands in the great majority with only a lone Daimler CVD6 in 1950 (HDK 80), two AECs in 1954 and 1966 (LDK 445, FDK 187D), and three Bedfords in 1962 and 1967 (two) (3017 DK, HDK 118/9E)

in addition to the two taken over with the Barnes business. In 1966 the two year old AEC, 449 GYV, with Harrington body, was hired in from London operator Fallowfield & Britten, part of the George Ewer Group. This covered the extended repairs to YDK 869 during the summer of 1966. The Harrington body fitted well into the fleet but no further information, nor a photograph, has come to light on this vehicle. Almost all mechanical and body work was carried out in-house. In the austerity days of 1947, when both chassis and bodies were in short supply, a 1933 Leyland Tiger TS4, (DK 8356), which had been requisitioned by the Army and returned in poor condition, was fitted with a Leyland diesel engine and its Roberts body replaced with a new body built in the Wardleworth garage by Jack Crabtree.

This vehicle then remained in service for another nine years. Leyland TS6 of 1934, DK 9092, was similarly rebodied, its Burlingham body being 13 years old, long past the time it would have been expected to last when it was built. This remained in the fleet for another 10 years in contrast to the two post-war Challenger bodies built on Tigers in 1948.

In the immediate post-war period new buses and coaches were not easy to come by. Consequently DK 9092, a Burlingham-bodied Leyland TS6 dating from 1934, by then 13 years old, was rebodied by Challenger in 1947. It gave a further ten years service before passing to Banfield Coaches of London in 1957. DK 9092 is pictured in its original condition, the official Burlingham photograph being dated 8th March 1934. *(EOC)*

Two Leyland PS1/1 Tigers, GDK 121 and GDK 122, were purchased in 1948, bodied by Jack Crabtree's Challenger company in Oldham to a design he had used on DK 9092 the previous year. In 1955 they were rebodied by Burlingham, and in this form remained in the fleet until 1964. GDK 121 is pictured (top) in its original condition and outside the garage (bottom) as rebodied. *(PGG; JJH)*

The second of the pair. GDK 122, proudly displays its Speedbird motif, a concession to modernity thought to have been inspired by Donald Campbell's water speed record attempts, although it was similar to BOAC's Speedbird logo. The two ladies standing by GDK 122 are Amy and Beryl, sisters of Betty, the wife of Eric Smith. Beryl is the wife of Jack Mills, a member of staff of the company. *(EOC)*

Although the majority of the post-war fleet was of Leyland origin, there were some exceptions. Daimler CVD6, HDK 80, was purchased in 1950 and remained in the fleet for eleven years. *(JJH)*

"LEYLAND"
Luxury Coaches.

ARE THE BEST AND MOST COMFORTABLE.

NOW that the dark days are over, your thoughts will soon be turning to your summer outing. We hope that you will let us help you in this, when the time is opportune.

We operate the most up-to-date super luxury coaches obtainable together with a staff of highly-competent drivers, who will do everything in their power to help you.

The coaches are of smart and striking appearance combined with beautifully toned interiors, luxuriously upholstered, which will help to make your outing all the more pleasant.

Let us have your enquiry. It will receive our best and immediate attention.

PERSONAL SUPERVISION IS GIVEN
—— TO ALL OUR PARTIES. ——

The last half-cab coach to join the fleet, HDK 236, a Leyland PS2/3 with Burlingham 33-seat body, served for 14 years before passing to an operator in the Republic of Ireland. Both views were taken at Wembley Stadium on different occasions. The upper photograph shows the coach in its original condition, whilst below it has lost its *Leyland Tiger* script badge from the radiator and has received modern headlamps whilst flashing trafficators have replaced the semaphore indicators. *(EOC; DNC)*

HDK 812, a 1951 Leyland PS2/3, was a unique vehicle in the fleet, this front-engined Tiger carrying a full-fronted Harrington body. Despite the attempt at modernity it retains semaphore direction indicators. In the upper picture it is parked outside Rochdale Town Hall, whilst across the Esplanade can be seen the steps of the cenotaph on the left and the General Post Office on the right. The old Hippodrome cinema in the background is long gone, being replaced by Lonsdale House, a 1960s concrete box housing government offices. The rear view, below, shows the famous and distinctive Harrington dorsal tail fin and the fleet name style on the boot doors painted by Jack Mills. *(BSC)*

Above: JDK 412, a 1952 Leyland PSU1/15 with Harrington 41-seat body, and Ellen Smith's first underfloor-engined Leyland Royal Tiger, is shown arriving at Wembley Stadium on hire to Walls of Wigan. Note the semaphore indicator in action. From 1952 to 1958 Ellen Smith's coaches featured a centre door. This was one of three or four coaches usually kept at Smallbridge garage, further along the road towards Littleborough. *(EOC)*

Below: KDK 1 was a Royal Tiger PSU1/16 delivered in 1953 with less decoration to its Harrington body. It has been updated with flashers fitted into the semaphore indicator recesses. A fault with this coach was that the driver's fingers could easily be caught between the steering wheel and the frame of the opening window, the latter being required by the regulations of the time. The registration number could be sold for a considerable sum today. *(DNC)*

Leyland Worldmaster

Harry Smith mentioned the time in the 1950s when Leyland was being difficult about accepting an order for normally export only Worldmasters. Introduced in 1954, this heavier version of the sturdy underfloor-engined Royal Tiger featured the 11.1 litre O.680 engine whereas the Royal Tiger's normal engine was the 9.8 litre O.600 version. When sales director Donald (later Lord) Stokes became aware of this he 'raised the roof' on the basis of 'looking after our oldest customers.' 'Within three days we had two chassis allocated,' said Harry. The Worldmasters certainly proved their worth as each one was rebodied by Plaxton after twelve years and went on to give another eleven and thirteen years front line service respectively (ODK 137, SDK 442). Eric Smith claimed that the company

had always received good service from Leyland and that he was well satisfied with the vehicles. He said that a well-maintained Leyland chassis would outlast the life of then current bodywork. Ever true to their staunch British principles the cousins ran British cars. Included among these were a black Austin A95 saloon, an Austin 3 litre Westminster (red) and a Ford Mark 4 Zephyr 6 (blue). A Vauxhall Viva (white) was bought for Marjorie which she never drove after being taught by 'father' Edgar Jenkinson. There were also some Rovers.

Around Easter time every year a travelling woman would engage with Harry with much gesticulating over the purchase of chamois leathers for cleaning the coach windows. The haggling over the price and quantity would go on for several hours with the woman sometimes departing and then returning to resume negotiations.

ODK 137, a 1956 Leyland RT3/1 with Plaxton body was the first of the two Royal Tiger Worldmaster chassis which Harry Smith had difficulty in obtaining until the intervention of Leyland's Donald Stokes as related in the text. Designed for overseas markets, it was Leyland's attempt to produce a world-wide chassis able to operate in extremes of climate and be equally efficient in city traffic and long distance touring. Fitted with the O.680 engine of 11.1-litres capacity, good performance was available at the expense of economy. Ellen Smith certainly achieved good service from this coach and SDK 442, since they went on to serve 23 and 25

years service respectively, albeit after rebodying. ODK 137 appeared in an article in Eagle comic when new. It is shown here with the new Plaxton Panorama body fitted in 1968. At the same time the chassis received a complete rewire in-house. All mechanical parts were upgraded including a higher ratio differential. It was used in alternate weeks during the season by Rochdale Hornets rugby league team and Rochdale association football team. Withdrawn in 1979 the chassis was exported by a later owner to the West Indies in 1983, the body having been scrapped after being wrecked by vandals. *(DNC)*

Above: For 1957 a Leyland Tiger Cub with Duple body was ordered. Realising that the Royal Tiger was over-engineered for British use, Leyland introduced a lighter weight version with the O.300 engine. Ellen Smith specified the four-speed crash gearbox and Eaton two-speed rear axle. RDK 4 lasted until 1974 when it was put out to grass for some years before passing to a dealer in 1985. *(EOC)*

Below: 1958 saw the arrival of SDK 442, the second Royal Tiger Worldmaster, again with a Plaxton 41-seat centre-door body, by now a Consort II. In 1970 it received a new Plaxton Panorama body and remained in service for a further 13 years before being withdrawn in 1983. It was later preserved and now resides in the Greater Manchester Transport Society Museum in Boyle Street, Manchester. *(EOC)*

Delivered in 1959, UDK 551 was a Leyland PSUC1/2 Tiger Cub with a Harrington 41-seat body. Ellen Smith standardised on Harrington bodies from 1959 until production ceased in 1965 and this was the first of the series. The original front panel was damaged at an early stage and the fibreglass front it carried for most of its life came from a Maidstone and District Tiger Cub. Maidstone and District operated a number of Harrington coaches and had Cavalier fronts fitted to them by the body builder, thus having spare front panels available. *(EOC)*

From 1947 to 1988 a new coach was purchased on average every year. This ensured that a new coach was always available for prestige jobs, continental private hires and other long journeys. Due to the standard of maintenance and presentation, and the reliability and quality of the Leyland chassis and engine, older coaches were always able to cope with all other work. Day excursions provided the main traffic.

Although this work was reducing generally within the industry, due to long experience, a regular following, and catering for customers' tastes, Ellen Smith had been able to maintain excursions at a profitable level. Imaginative destinations played a significant part in the success of excursions for which the author can vouch, with trips to London, Edinburgh and the Motor Shows at Earls Court and the National Exhibition Centre.

The 1960s

A regular excursion in the 1960s and 1970s was a tour of London Airport, usually driven by Eric and a front-line co-driver. The tour involved a drive round the 13 miles of perimeter road with an airport guide, visits afterwards to the observation areas, booking halls, restaurants, bars and shops, concluding with an evening meal at Watford Gap on the return journey. Excursions to historic houses were a speciality, and holiday tours were operated extending from Scotland to the South West of England, ranging in duration from a weekend to eight days.

Ellen Smith attained national recognition in 1961 when driver 'young' Edgar Jenkinson won Coach Driver of the Year at the seventh British Coach Rally held in Brighton on 23rd April, driving Leyland Leopard YDK 869 with a Harrington 41-seat body. One of 67 entries from all parts of Britain, the Leyland Journal stated that 'he put up a remarkable performance against many seasoned rally drivers in tests which observers claimed to be the toughest ever held in this country or on the continent.'

Aged 29, it was only his second appearance in a coach rally. The rally consisted of a 94-mile road section from London to Brighton on the Saturday which included a 15-mile regularity test, eliminating

XDK 279 was a 1960 Leyland L1T with Harrington 41-seat body. Leyland introduced the new medium weight Leopard to fill the gap between the lightweight Tiger Cub and the heavyweight Royal Tiger Worldmaster in 1959, the home-market Royal Tiger having ceased production in 1955. With progressive development the Leopard remained in production for over 20 years, providing operators with both good performance and economy. XDK 279 had a low differential allowing a speed of 60mph. It was Ellen Smith's first Leopard and its first Cavalier body. Withdrawn in 1977 it ended its life as a stock car transporter. *(EOC)*

YDK 869 was a Leopard L2T with a Harrington 41-seat body delivered in 1961. *(DNC)*

A Leyland Leopard PSU3/3RT of 1962, 3161 DK was Ellen Smith's first coach to the new length of 36ft following revision of the Construction and Use Regulations, allowing a seating capacity of 51 in the Harrington Cavalier body. Originally supplied with a low ratio Eaton 2-speed rear axle, it was retrofitted with a higher 3:1 ratio axle. *(EOC)*

Two further Leopards came in 1963. 4728 DK was fitted with 45 Chapman reclining seats and weighed almost a ton more than its sisters. 6733 DK, pictured below, had 49 seats and a high ratio differential from new, but suffered from extremely heavy steering. In 1979 it passed to Classique Sun Saloon Luxury Coaches of Paisley. The registration number was later transferred to an ex-Glenton coach. It is related that this coach was once chased by a police car that had difficulty keeping up with it. When the driver stopped at the services the policemen simply wanted to inspect the engine, as they were astonished by its turn of speed. This was, of course, before motorway speed limits were introduced. *(PGG)*

YDK 869 was entered in the 1961 British Coach Rally at Brighton, driven by 'young' Edgar Jenkinson, who was successful in winning the Coach Driver of the Year and was runner-up in the Concours Class. The pictures show, opposite page top, Edgar competing in the eliminating driving tests in torrential rain, above Harry Smith receiving the trophy from Lord Montagu of Beaulieu and opposite page bottom Edgar driving away in the garlanded coach. *(DNC; Leyland Journal; BSC)*

tests for acceleration, braking, reversing, parking, quick starting and manoeuvrability to reduce the field to eight, and three final exhaustive tests the next day. Trophies were presented to the driver and Harry Smith by Lord Montagu of Beaulieu. A somewhat embarrassing incident occurred before this presentation. Ken Barker had specially tuned the engine of the coach for the final run-off. While other waiting competitors had switched off their engines, Ken kept Edgar's engine running fast. Consequently, when it came Edgar's turn to make a quick getaway from the 'box,' his front wheels lifted from the ground. As he accelerated hard after the long tickover, the exhaust emitted smoke and soot which enveloped the VIPs including the Mayor of Brighton!

The business of Benjamin Barnes & Son of Wood Top Garage, Holme Bank, Rawtenstall was purchased in 1964, thus expanding the operational area and enabling a travel shop to be opened in the town. The coaches, being non-Leylands, were sold off except for two Leyland-engined Bedford SB5s (539/40 XTF), which remained in the fleet for three years. They were noisy to drive in comparison with the Leylands and were part-exchanged in 1967 for two new Bedford VAM 14s (HDK 118/9E) which lasted in the fleet for five years.

On the purchase of the Benjamin Barnes business, the two Bedford coaches were garaged in the premises of a local undertakers and Ellen Smith retained this outstation for two years. Ernest Ormerod and Clifford Nicholas were the two drivers taken over with the business. Sometimes coffins would be inside the garage and this always made Clifford very nervous. One night Ernest garaged his coach and lay down inside a coffin to await Clifford's arrival. At the appropriate moment, Ernest emerged from the coffin in the darkness causing Clifford to flee the premises in fright!

A feature of the company of which the directors were proud was that everything owned, premises and vehicles, were fully paid for on purchase without resorting to credit.

A notable refurbishment by Plaxton was that of 1965 Leyland Leopard CDK 448C in 1984, the last Harrington body purchased before that quality builder ceased production in 1966. This splendid coach then returned to full time service before withdrawal in 1986 in its 21st year. It was still owned at the time of the sale of the business in 1991 and then passed to Rothwells of Heywood, who later sold it into preservation. By 2006 it was with a Mr Rogers of Kidderminster and appears on the rally circuit.

CDK 448C, a 1965 Leyland PSU3/3RT, was the last of Ellen Smith's Harrington-bodied Leopards. The quality coachbuilder ceased production that year, a fact regretted by many top class operators such as Southdown, the George Ewer Group, Yelloway and, of course, Ellen Smith. The body was fully refurbished in 1984 but subsequently saw little use due to an ongoing engine fault. CDK 448C was retained by Eric Smith on the sale of the company in 1991 who later sold it to Barry Ribchester, the proprietor of nearby Rothwell's Coaches of Heywood. It later passed into preservation and by 2006 was with a Mr Rogers of Kidderminster. (EOC)

The Leopard for 1967 was this Plaxton Panorama bodied PSU3/4RT model, HDK 751E. It featured in an article in the August 1967 edition of the *Leyland Journal* on an excursion to London's Heathrow Airport, as pictured on page 58. This coach was involved in a serious accident at Holywell in North Wales which resulted in it being rebodied for the 1975 season. The driver swerved to avoid a car, which had driven into his path and the coach ran down an embankment, remaining on its wheels but at an angle. Fortunately, there were no injuries but the body was badly damaged and was brought home; engine vibration was cured by the simple expedient of breaking off a fan blade opposite to one broken in the accident. Both bodies are shown here, the old one in the upper picture and the new one in the lower. *(DNC; EOC)*

On the demise of Harrington, Plaxton of Scarborough became Ellen Smith's favoured coachbuilder and two coaches were delivered in 1966. FDK 94D (opposite page top) was once again a Leyland Leopard PSU3/3RT model. This 49-seat Panorama I coach was entered in the 1966 Brighton Rally but failed to win anything after the company's previous success there. In the same year, however, it won the Paignton Hotel Association Cup. After 19 years service it was sold to a jazz band in Hyde in 1985. The photograph shows it when new. *(DNC)*

The other 1966 delivery (opposite page bottom) was FDK 187D, another rare departure from Leyland in the shape of an AEC Reliance, this time with the shorter 41-seat body. The photograph shows it parked outside the garage in 1981, unfortunately with a scrap yard in the background. It was described as a good coach which served the company well, but as with many AEC 470 engines, it suffered gasket problems in later life. It must have given satisfaction, however, as it remained in the fleet for 20 years. FDK 187D ended its life in the undignified role of a stock car transporter. *(EO)*

With two similar bodies on different chassis bought in the same year, this may have been an experiment to compare the two makes. Though both gave lengthy service, Ellen Smith remained with the Leyland marque, perhaps because of their good relationship with Leyland Motors and Donald (later Lord) Stokes.

In 1967 two Leyland O.400-engined Bedford VAM14s, HDK 118E and HDK 119E, were purchased to replace the five year old Bedford SB5s retained when the business of Benjamin Barnes was acquired in 1964. They were based at Barnes's former Wood Top garage in Rawtenstall. Both coaches were withdrawn in 1972, passing to Moxon of Oldcotes, Nottinghamshire. HDK 118E is pictured above when new. *(DNC)*

No coaches were purchased in 1968 but new for 1969 was this Plaxton Elite-bodied Leopard PSU4/4RT, NDK 18G, which served for 19 years. It was the first of four coaches originally fitted with all-leather seats and was sold for preservation in 1988. *(EOC)*

The 1970s and 1980s

Alan Schofield recalled driving the chassis of PDK 829M in 1974 with a temporary seat and windshield and wearing waterproofs and a crash helmet in the manner of trade journal road testers of the time. He drove the chassis from Leyland to Rochdale, then to the Plaxton works at Scarborough where it was found that Plaxton could not guarantee completion for the start of the season. So Alan drove it back to Rochdale and next day to the Duple works at Blackpool where the vehicle was bodied in time for the season's work. He was relieved to drive back to Rochdale in a brand new complete coach! Alan commenced with Ellen Smith in 1965 and went on to drive coaches through the Rossendale Transport period and into Paul Targett's present operation. Usually, whoever was to have the following year's coach drove the chassis to the coachbuilder. Eric Smith drove PDK 829M from new.

From 1967 to 1988 only Leylands were bought, Leopards, Tigers and finally the two Royal Tiger Doyens. The standard body was now the Plaxton, only two Duples joining the fleet in 1974 and 1981 (PDK 829M, FTD 758W). The latter suffered initial problems with the hydraulics on the ZF auto gearbox. Alan Schofield's adventures with the former have been related earlier and it is significant that no more Duples were purchased, especially since Duple's Blackpool works was much closer to Ellen Smith's Rochdale base than Plaxton at Scarborough.

The flagships of the fleet came in the form of the two Leyland Royal Tiger Doyens and they turned out to be the last vehicles purchased. This was Leyland's attempt to compete with the best continental coaches which by the 1980s were proving increasingly attractive to British operators. Hitherto, operators had been wary of integral coaches but the continentals were gaining ground, not least Volvo and Scania with several

European body builders, notably Van Hool and Jonckheere. Top of the range were the German Setra and Neoplan integrals and it became essential for Leyland to attempt to enter this market. Starting from scratch it built a rear-engined spaceframe underframe which carried a Leyland designed 12-metre body to produce a semi-integral coach of impressive appearance with a huge one-piece windscreen and bonded glazing. Early examples were built at the Roe factory in Leeds, then owned by Leyland, but after questionable build quality and teething troubles, especially problems with the fit of the main door, production was switched to the Leyland National bus factory in Workington in 1983. Quality was then greatly improved but the door problems were never entirely eliminated. The Ellen Smith examples were D892 PNB, a 53-seater in 1987, and D387 VAO, also seating 53, a former demonstrator built in 1987 and purchased in 1988.

The earlier Doyen was painted in Ellen Smith livery of red and white with the famous Leaping Tiger and a large fleetname, while the other retained its demo livery of light grey, red and black with large Leyland logo on the sides to the end of Smith family operation. On passing to the Rossendale fleet both were repainted and a new style Tiger was applied thus breaking a tradition of 60 years. Both Doyens passed from the Rossendale fleet to Stephenson's Coaches of Rochford, near Southend Airport in Essex. One was used by Stephensons for regular journeys to Spain 'without any serious problems.' Doyen D387 VAO (by then OIB 5402) was acquired by TM Travel of Halfway near Sheffield at the same time as two others as preservation projects. Unfortunately, it was past reasonable repair and has now been passed to a dealer for scrap following the takeover TM Travel by the Wellglade Group. Had Leyland continued in existence, the Royal Tiger Doyen could have been developed into a successful and desirable top-grade coach and a common sight on British and continental roads. In the event only 98 complete vehicles were built and another 65 underframes were bodied by Plaxton and Van Hool after six million pounds had been spent on development and building facilities. The fact that Ellen Smith operated two of them was no doubt due to the cousins' enthusiasm for Leyland products and the good relationship and long association enjoyed with the manufacturer. It was regrettable that Ellen Smith did not survive long enough to obtain the full benefit from these impressive vehicles, some of which went on to give long service with other operators. Marjorie Smith said that had they not sold the business they would have bought two new coaches in 1991. One wonders whether they would have been Doyens.

PDK 763H was a Plaxton 49-seat bodied Leopard PSU3A/4RT. Delivered in 1970 it served for 18 years. It was photographed in August 1984 behind the garage alongside rebodied HDK 751E. *(EO)*

Above: Delivered in 1971, TDK 594J was a Leopard PSU3B/4RT model with Plaxton 51-seat body. Harry Smith and Douglas Neal drove with the Leyland representative to Scarborough to collect this coach from the Plaxton works on 21st May 1971. This was Douglas's coach until he left in March 1973 and in those 22 months it covered 85,450 miles, an average of 3,884 miles a month. In the first eighteen weeks he covered 25,260 miles, an average of 1,403 miles a week or 200 a day! *(EO)*

Below: Another Plaxton-bodied Leopard that remained in the fleet for 18 years was WDK 916K. Withdrawn in 1990, it passed to Bolton operator Holt Driver, who hired it to Bolton School in 1990, which continues to run its own fleet of coaches. *(EO)*

Both these photographs were taken outside the Wardleworth garage. The front office on the right hand side was known as the red office, from its interior décor, until it was demolished by SDK 442 in 1964. The driver left it in gear as he revved the engine to build up air pressure, causing the coach to leap forward and collide with the office. The several Smith cats flew out of the broken front window! The lean-to office attached to the left hand side of the garage was built by Ken Barker and the drivers during the winter lull and became the main office, the repaired red office being used as a store.

A second new coach in 1972 was 12-metre Leopard PSU5/4RT YDK 165L. Its Plaxton body contained 57 seats and it was fitted with an engine exhaust brake. This coach is shown in the upper photograph in May 1989 at the Saddleworth Whit Friday Brass Band Contest, in Lydgate, one of several villages in which the bands play their contest pieces. The leaping tiger is temporarily absent. *(EO)*

The lower view shows the coach in March 1991 after the business was sold to municipally-owned Rossendale Transport Ltd. A paper sheet showing Rossendale's legal lettering is affixed over the Ellen Smith name and the vehicle is on hire to Peter Cartmel's Border Tours of Burnley at whose premises it is parked. It later passed to Evans of Tregaron. *(NO)*

Opposite page top: Following local government re-organisation in 1974, County Borough councils such as Rochdale were abolished and with them their vehicle licensing offices. Registration letters were then allocated to a number of Driver and Vehicle Licensing Agency offices, which meant that Ellen Smith could no longer automatically receive former Rochdale registrations in the DK series. Bolton became the new licensing office covering Rochdale, using several of the former registration letters in its area. This Plaxton-bodied 57-seat Leyland Leopard was delivered in 1975 carrying former Lancashire County Council registration number HTD 589N. Douglas Neal delivered this coach new from Plaxton. It passed from Rossendale Transport to a dealer in 1994. This picture was taken in May 1985 in Lydgate, one of the Saddleworth villages hosting the annual Whit Friday Brass Band Contest. *(EO)*

Opposite page bottom: Plaxton-bodied 57-seat Leyland Leopard LCB 652P was again registered in Bolton using former Blackburn letters and carried an earlier Leyland plate. This 1976 Leopard continued the fleet standard, but the Plaxton Supreme body wears a revised livery style considered to be more modern. *(JJH)*

Above. The next four coaches were registered in Scotland, the reason being unclear. It was said that Harry Smith wished to obtain the Scottish registration letters EST (Ellen Smith Tours) since Rochdale's DK was no longer normally available. Having made the arrangements for registration in Scotland the idea failed and subsequent registrations took Glasgow and Edinburgh letters. Another theory was that a Scottish dealer was involved. This photograph of UGG 369R, a 1977 Plaxton-bodied 53-seat Leopard PSU3C/4R, was taken on the occasion of a trip to Sheffield's Meadowhall Shopping Centre on 26th January 1991, perhaps the family company's final day excursion. The well-known double-deck Tinsley viaduct on the M1 motorway and one of the famous power station cooling towers, since demolished, are visible in the background. Rossendale Transport sold UGG 369R to a dealer in 1993. *(EO)*

Continuing the Scottish theme 1978s coach, a Leopard PSU5B/4R with 53-seat Plaxton body, was registered CFS 264S. It is photographed behind the garage. Rossendale Transport passed it to Peter Cartmel's Border Tours of Burnley and from there in 1997 it went to Abbot of Leeming in North Yorkshire for further service. *(EOC)*

Photographed at the garage in October 1988 is LFS 487T, a 1979 Leopard PSU3E/4R with 49-seat Plaxton body. This coach was re-registered OIB 3608 by Rossendale before passing to Border Tours in 1996 and then to a dealer in 1998. *(EO)*

40

1980 saw the arrival of UFS 690V, a Leopard PSU5C/5R with the now-standard Plaxton body, this time seating 53. The upper view was taken in February 1981, also showing the office attached to the garage, mentioned on page 37. This was the author's parking spot when on the excursions. The picture below shows the coach looking just as smart nearly ten years later in December 1990. Re-registered OIB 6207 by Rossendale Transport, it went to Border Tours in 1996, then to a Norfolk operator for further service in 1999. *(EO both)*

The 1981 Rochdale Holidays programme, covering Sunday, 21st June to Sunday, 5th July (no Saturdays due to the holiday expresses on that day) offered around ten different day excursions each day. There were many varied and enterprising destinations such as Loch Lomond, Hunstanton, London, Isle of Anglesey, Bamburgh Castle, the Cotswolds, Edinburgh, Windsor, the Wye Valley, Snowdonia, Weston-Super-Mare and the Trossachs in addition to the more local excursions to the Lancashire, Yorkshire and North Wales coastal resorts.

In the 1980s Ellen Smith participated in a summer daily express coach service from Oldham to Morecambe together with the other major Rochdale coach operator, Yelloway Motor Services Ltd. Service X50 linked Oldham, Rochdale and the surrounding towns with the seaside resort, covering also Lancaster and Pontins Holiday Camp at Middleton Towers. There was also a weekly holiday service to Scarborough and the Yorkshire coastal resorts at this time.

The Smiths sold retail fuel from the pumps at the garage. The diesel pump was at the corner requiring the vehicle to be parked at the side of the garage. Some taxi drivers thought they were out of sight of the office and switched off the pump before taking more fuel in a second fill and paying only for the latter. This was soon stopped as unknown to the miscreant, Harry could see the reflection in the window. After detaining the offender until he paid in full, the word went round and the practice ceased.

In 1985, a 1974 Duple Dominant-bodied Leopard, PDK 829M was returned to the coachbuilder's Blackpool factory for re-panelling, re-trimming and the fitting of a new floor. Later, two further coaches were similarly treated at the Duple factory. All spray repainting was carried out in the garage by Ken Barker. For example, in 1967, XDK 279 was largely re-panelled for its seven-year Certificate of Fitness (as was required at the time) and Ken Barker sprayed it in its entirety. He treated other coaches as they came up for C.O.F. Any brush painting, such as replacement panels, the gilt scrolls on the rears and the legal lettering was done by Jack Mills who hand painted the Leaping Tiger crests.

Leyland's Tiger succeeded the Leopard and in 1981 FTD 758W was Ellen Smith's first Tiger coach, a TRCTL11/3R model. In another departure it was fitted with a Duple Dominant body. Rossendale Transport re-registered it OIB 8606 and sold it to Timeline of Leigh in 1994. Taken over by Arriva in 1998 it passed to a Maidstone operator. *(EOC)*

The Tiger was now the standard chassis and in 1983 FJA 400Y marked a return to Plaxton bodies. The Paramount was recognised by the small feature window part way along the body. Re-registered OIB 6205, this coach passed from Rossendale Transport to Owls Coaches of Long Ditton, Surrey in 1999. *(JJH)*

Introducing the year prefix to registrations into the fleet A886 OND, a further Plaxton-bodied Tiger, came in 1984. It is pictured here at London's Earls Court in October 1989. *(EO)*

Also received in 1984 was the fleet's final Leyland Tiger with Plaxton Paramount body. This picture was taken at Manchester University in December 1986 with Eric Smith at the wheel. Later re-registered OIB 5403, this was the last Ellen Smith coach to remain with Rossendale where it joined the separate Coachways fleet, passing to a dealer in 2002. *(EO)*

Harry Smith died aged 74 on 29th May 1988. He had joined the firm on leaving school at the age of 14 and was still actively engaged with the company after sixty years. He had run the company with his cousin Eric since the early 1970s.

Harry's widow, Marjorie, then became more involved, running the office, and working with Eric until the sale of the company to Rossendale Transport in 1991.

Harry and Marjorie were never known to take a holiday. It is said that a holiday for Marjorie was a day out at Scarborough – to visit the Plaxton factory!

The one exception to this was a 6-week visit to New Zealand in the 1970s. Harry spoke of seeing a Worldmaster like one of his own during the stopover in Singapore.

Harry was one of those bosses who, if a driver arrived with a dirty coach late at night after a long journey, would help the driver to wash it. He was also known to help a driver financially if in need.

Throughout 1989 there were holiday tours of between three and eight days based on such centres as Torquay, Folkestone, Eastbourne, the Isle of Wight, Newquay, Blairgowrie, Llandudno, Bournemouth and Whitby. There were also long weekends in London (Tower Hotel) and Edinburgh (King James Hotel) and an eight day tour to the Republic of Ireland. These were imaginative programmes indeed for a 14-vehicle operator. Despite the success of these tours they were never encouraged by Marjorie. She is quoted as saying "the amount of paperwork for just one tour doesn't make it a viable proposition." Marjorie, of course, ran the office more or less on her own with just the help of, first, Joan Bostock, and later Doreen Rawlinson, whose husband Frank was a driver.

Eric Smith explained the Lancashire Wakes holiday tradition whereby local towns took a week's holiday (later two weeks) in turn, starting in mid-June. This originated in the days of the extensive Lancashire cotton industry which had all but ceased by 1990. It was the one occasion in the year when the mill and engineering workers enjoyed a break from the grinding routine of work in the mills and factories.

It was the highlight of the year for them. As one town's holiday finished another one started. Ellen Smith's catchment area was such that one or more towns were on holiday throughout the summer to the end of September. This provided excursion traffic during the week serving those who took

Leyland Royal Tiger Doyen D892 PNB (upper) was registered on April Fool's Day 1987. The Doyen was Leyland's attempt to compete with the top-flight continental manufacturers and was the start of the Leyland presence at the Coach and Bus Show held at the National Exhibition centre in Birmingham in October 1986. After purchase by Rossendale Transport it was re-registered OIB 5401 and passed to Stephenson of Rochford, Essex in 1993, along with sister vehicle D387 VAO (lower). *(JJH)*

The second Doyen to be purchased was a former Leyland demonstrator built at the Leyland National factory at Workington. New in 1987, it joined the fleet the following year, its demonstration livery being retained until its transfer to Rossendale. This view shows the troublesome door which affected most Doyens. *(EO)*

ELLEN SMITH (TOURS) LTD.

Daily Express Coach Services

MORECAMBE/SOUTHPORT
— LANCASTER —
MIDDLETON TOWERS

— AINSDALE —

To & From OLDHAM—SHAW—ROCHDALE—HEYWOOD—BURY—BOLTON

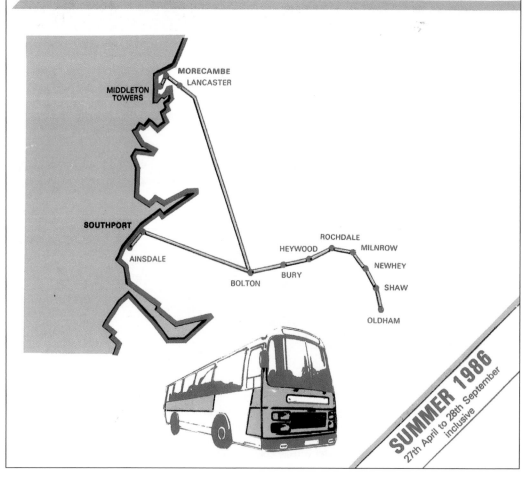

In the summer of 1986 express services to Morecambe and Southport were operated jointly with Yelloway Motor Services Ltd under network route numbers X50 and X51. Only Morecambe was operated the following year. *(DN)*

SERVICE NUMBER	X50	X50	X50	X51	X51
PERIOD OF OPERATION (Both Dates inclusive)	27 April to 18 May	24 May to 28 Sept.	25 May to 28 Sept.	25 May to 28 Sept.	24 May to 28 Sept.
DAYS OF OPERATION	SSu	S	NS	NS	S
OLDHAM .... Yelloway Coach Station 3 Mumps	0900	0900	0900	0930	0930
SHAW .... 40 Market Street	0910	0910	0910	0940	0940
NEWHEY .... Newhey Road	0915	0915	0915	0945	0945
MILNROW .... Bridge Street	0919	0919	0919	0949	0949
FIRGROVE .... 175 Rochdale Road	0921	0921	0921	0951	0951
ROCHDALE .... E. Smith, Wardleworth Garage	0927	0927	0927	0957	0957
ROCHDALE .... E. Smith, Newgate	0930	0930	0930	1000	1000
ROCHDALE .... Yelloway Coach Station, Weir St.	0935	0935	0935	1005	1005
HEYWOOD .... Happidays Travel Bureau, Market Street ...	0946	0946	0946	1016	1016
BURY .... Moss Street	0957	0957	0957	1027	1027
RADCLIFFE .... opposite Three Arrows	1003	1003	1003	1033	1033
BOLTON .... Moor Lane Bus Station	1015	1015	1015	1045	1045
LOSTOCK .... opposite Bee Hive Hotel	1027	1027	1027	1057	1057
LANCASTER .... Damside Street Bus Station	1118	1118	1118	↓	↓
MORECAMBE .... Euston Road Bus Station	1130	1130	1130		
MIDDLETON TOWERS ..... Pontins Camp		1142			
SOUTHPORT .... Bus Station	–	–	–	1154	1154
AINSDALE .... Pontins Camp	–	–	–		1209

SERVICE NUMBER	X51	X51	X50	X50	X50
PERIOD OF OPERATION (Both Dates inclusive)	24 May to 28 Sept.	24 May to 28 Sept.	27 April to 18 May	24 May to 28 Sept.	25 May to 28 Sept.
DAYS OF OPERATION	S	NS	SSu	S	NS
AINSDALE .... Pontins Camp	1300		–	–	–
SOUTHPORT .... Bus Station	1315	1800	–		–
MIDDLETON TOWERS ..... Pontins Camp	↓	↓		1310	
MORECAMBE .... Euston Road Bus Station			1830	1330	1830
LANCASTER .... Damside Street Bus Station			1845	1345	1845
LOSTOCK .... near Bee Hive Hotel	1412	1857	1936	1436	1936
BOLTON .... Moor Lane Bus Station	1424	1909	1948	1448	1948
RADCLIFFE .... Three Arrows	1433	1918	1957	1457	1957
BURY .... Moss Street	1439	1924	2003	1503	2003
HEYWOOD .... Happidays Travel Bureau, Market Street ...	1441	1935	2014	1514	2014
ROCHDALE .... E. Smith, Newgate	1451	1945	2024	1524	2024
ROCHDALE .... Yelloway Coach Station, Weir Street......	1454	1948	2027	1527	2027
ROCHDALE .... E. Smith, Wardleworth Garage	1457	1951	2030	1530	2030
FIRGROVE .... opposite 175 Rochdale Road	1503	1957	2036	1536	2036
MILNROW .... Bridge Street	1505	1959	2038	1538	2038
NEWHEY .... Newhey Road	1509	2003	2042	1542	2042
SHAW .... opposite 40 Market Street	1514	2008	2047	1547	2047
OLDHAM .... Yelloway Coach Station, 3 Mumps	1524	2018	2057	1557	2057

CODE: SSu – SATURDAYS & SUNDAY ONLY   S – SATURDAY   NS – DAILY EXCEPT SATURDAY

BOOK YOUR PONTINS HOLIDAY AT MIDDLETON TOWERS OR AINSDALE
– THE EASY WAY THROUGH YELLOWAY –
AT THEIR OFFICES IN ROCHDALE, BURY OR OLDHAM.

'holidays at home' (a wartime slogan which continued into the immediate post-war years of austerity) and weekend return trips to and from the coast for holidaymakers in the traditional resorts such as Blackpool, Morecambe and Scarborough. Excursions covered the traditional destinations such as the Lancashire coast, the Yorkshire resorts and North Wales. During the Wakes Weeks the West Yorkshire towns of Todmorden and Hebden Bridge were covered in addition to the Rochdale and Oldham areas. A few drivers actually lived in these West Yorkshire areas.

Private hire was always preferred (especially by Marjorie) since it avoided work concerned with planning excursions, arranging the advertising and dealing with agents. Ellen Smith arranged its excursions around the private hire bookings depending on the vehicles available. Even so, demand sometimes outstripped the fleet size and coaches would then be hired in on reciprocal arrangements with other operators. On a summer day in 1990 Eric Smith told a journalist that 22 coaches were out, his full fleet of 14 plus eight hired in.

Eric Smith's main form of advertising was regular inserts in the local newspapers. This method kept the familiar name to the forefront for readers throughout the company's catchment area. The travel office in Rochdale's Newgate sold tickets for the local and very popular operatic society which brought people into the shop and would perhaps plant the seed that it would be a good idea to take an excursion if not a holiday tour. In any case, passers-by in the town centre would be made aware of what was on offer. The smart red and white vehicles seen about the town were an advertisement in themselves, instantly recognisable as Ellen Smith coaches, a name most townspeople had always known. These factors combined to create a high profile in Rochdale and the surrounding towns which was reflected in the high take-up of seats within the programme.

In 1989 Eric Smith was talking of his company having a good future but it was announced at the beginning of January 1991 that Ellen Smith (Tours) Ltd was to be sold to Rossendale Transport Ltd, the council-owned local bus company, at the end of the month. Rossendale, based in Rawtenstall, also served Rochdale and operated a number of coaches alongside its bus fleet. Eric and Marjorie had decided to retire and there was no one to whom they could pass on the business. They looked for a buyer with a long history, a good reputation and a sound financial background, with a guarantee of employment for the 20 staff. The company was to remain a separate entity, a wholly-owned subsidiary of Rossendale Transport Ltd. Thirteen of the 14 coaches were included in the sale but not the Wardleworth garage, CDK 448C being retained and sold separately. This was later sold to the tyre-fitting company ATS. Rossendale Transport already had a Rochdale sub-depot in Corporation Road and the new Ellen Smith headquarters was based at the Newgate office in the town centre. The booking office in Bury Road, Rawtenstall was also included in the sale. Leonard Green, managing director of Rossendale Transport, became managing director of Ellen Smith, and Eric and Marjorie Smith continued for a time as part-time consultants. Eric died aged 77 on 17th October 2000. Douglas Neal was appointed joint manager of both coach fleets until he resigned in August 1991.

The end! A paper label showing the new legal lettering is taped over the Ellen Smith lettering on 23rd March 1991. *(EO)*

Rossendale Transport

ossendale Transport's new subsidiary continued its normal business of excursions, tours and private hire for the next eleven years, and new and good second-hand coaches gradually replaced the final Ellen Smith fleet. Rossendale already operated a 12-strong coach fleet and at first the Ellen Smith fleet was kept separate.

By 1994, however, the two coach units had become integrated with a total fleet strength of 35. A new image was launched with a new livery style retaining the familiar red and white colours and the Leaping Tiger. New high class coaches for the 'Grand Luxe' standard were introduced including nine Van Hool executives. Six of them operated 92 tour departures throughout the year including a Spanish programme serving six resorts, and Easter in Paris. Amsterdam and Jersey by air were also offered in 1993. Door-to-door service with a Volkswagen Caravelle and Ford Galaxy, breakfast en route, top quality hotels and premium day excursions were offered on the new tour programme.

There was local speculation in 1996 that the Ellen Smith subsidiary, along with the parent company, was to be sold but this was denied by the municipal company's chairman. However, by 2002 the coaching unit was losing money and the decision was taken to sell in a management buy-out to two directors of the subsidiary, John White and Paul Targett. John White is a member of the family which owned the coach company E T White & Sons Ltd, White's Travel, of Calver in Derbyshire. He was appointed tours manager at Ellen Smith in 1995 shortly after White's was acquired by the municipal company Chesterfield Transport Ltd which was later taken over by the Stagecoach Group. Since Stagecoach was not interested in excursions and tours, Rossendale took the opportunity to acquire this side of White's business using the Whiteway Tours fleetname. The operation was moved to Buxton which provided an outstation for Ellen Smith. A coach was kept there together with a Volkswagen Caravelle for use as a feeder to the motorway pick-up point for holiday tours. John White was promoted to executive director of Ellen Smith (Tours) Ltd in 2000 when he became responsible for the tours programme and the six travel shops including that at Buxton. Another subsidiary company, ABTA-bonded Estelle Travel Centres Ltd, the name of which was formed from the initial letters of Ellen Smith (Tours), was set up to operate the travel shops. In 2002 John White and Paul Targett, Rossendale's finance director, purchased Ellen Smith (Tours) Ltd as a management buy-out from Rossendale Transport Ltd. The deal covered five coaches and five travel shops in Rochdale (2), Bury, Middleton and Buxton. The Rawtenstall outlet was retained by Rossendale Transport Ltd. All staff employed

Rossendale 307, a 1980 Plaxton-bodied Leopard formerly Ellen Smith UFS 690V, is pictured at Lydgate on a Whit Friday private hire in June 1993. It passed to Border Coaches of Burnley in 1996 and was with a Norfolk operator by 1999. *(EO)*

Plaxton-bodied Leyland Tiger OIB 3604 was originally Ellen Smith A886 OND. It is pictured on a private hire to Oldham's Coliseum Theatre on Christmas Eve 1994. It remained in the fleet until 1999. *(NO)*

OIB 5402, the former Leyland Royal Tiger Doyen demonstrator, stands in Rossendale's Rochdale yard, numbered 302 and freshly painted into Ellen Smith colours in 1991. *(JJH)*

Rossendale 319 E329 OMG was a 1988 Volvo B10M with Van Hool 51-seat body. This popular coach operators 'workhorse' combination was acquired from nearby Rothwell of Heywood in whose livery it is seen with the addition of the Ellen Smith fleet name. It was repainted into Ellen Smith livery and re-registered NIW 6519 in 1994 and passed to Berwyn of Trefor, North Wales in 1999. *(MB via HP)*

N300 EST, a 1996 Plaxton-bodied Dennis Javelin, was purchased new and painted in the Ellen Smith livery for the new brand Elite Tours, It remained in the Rossendale fleet on the sale of the Ellen Smith subsidiary. The registration represents Ellen Smith Tours. Dennis was a late entrant into the coach chassis market and its products were comparatively rare. *(EO)*

in the Ellen Smith operation transferred to the new company which rented part of Rossendale's Rochdale premises and yard in Corporation Road. John White retired in 2006 leaving Paul Targett as sole director.

Rossendale Transport retained some coaches for a new operation under the name Coachways Ltd. This catered for private hire and school trips to France, Germany and Spain on behalf of Rhapsody Tours, and contracted tours for other tour companies such as Travelsphere of Market Harborough and Northern Tours of Middleton, Manchester. There was also a weekly coach to the Costa Brava resorts in Spain operated by Sunways Direct Holidays. Edgar Oldham, current managing director of Rossendale Transport, said that the sale of the Ellen Smith subsidiary would be of mutual benefit to enable both companies to concentrate on their core businesses.

The coaches inherited by the new Ellen Smith company from the Rossendale operation were gradually replaced with new vehicles commencing in 2003 with a Beulas-bodied Iveco (FG03 JDU). A Mercedes -Benz Touro followed in 2004 (BX54 EBA), followed by two Bovas in 2005 and 2007 (YJ55 EYV, YJ57 EYS). These are said to 'make a big impression' on the customers in the new striking black livery with the large tiger head.

The current holiday tours programme (2009) continues with imaginative destinations along with the tried and tested traditional British resorts which continue to appeal to the Rochdale, Oldham and Bury people. As many as 27 departures a month take place between April and October. European destinations include Paris, Germany, the Austrian Tyrol, the Italian Riviera and the Republic of Ireland. Home destinations cover England, Wales, Scotland, Northern Ireland, Jersey and Guernsey. Over 10,000 customers are carried each year in the most modern coaches and a door to door service is offered using Volkswagen Caravelles and taxis. Day excursions continue to be offered.

When owned by the Smith family, the 75 years of motor vehicle operation covered the history of coaching from early interchangeable goods and passenger chassis, mostly Leyland, to the best of their day, the Leyland Royal Tiger Doyens.

The tradition which they set of service and quality continues today with top-flight modern coaches and personal service. Ellen Smith on her Littleborough farm could not have believed that her name would live on into the 21st century.

Four Bova FHD12 integral coaches were delivered to Rossendale in 1999 as T341-4 NBV. Three were painted in Ellen Smith Livery and 341 was in the blue of Northern Holidays. The four coaches, seen here on delivery from Moseley, were the first foreign coaches to carry the Ellen Smith name. From the left are Barry Drelincourt (Operations Director, Rossendale), Terry Flanagan (Moseley) and Paul Mason (Commercial Director, Ellen Smith (Tours) Ltd). *(EOC)*

Rossendale 389 LIW 4289 was a Plaxton-bodied Tiger originally new to London Country Bus Services as TPL48, passing to Kentish Bus when LCBS was broken up into separate operating companies. It was acquired by Rossendale and is seen at Oldham Mumps in June 1996. (EOC)

ELLEN SMITH

LIW 4289

Information

Excursions and Tours

Ellen Smith built up their coaching business after the First World War using lorries with demountable bodies. The lorry body was taken off and replaced with a charabanc body at weekends and public holidays to carry passengers for days out to the seaside and other scenic destinations. These primitive vehicles were soon superseded by purpose-built charabancs such as DK 5053, a Burlingham-bodied Leyland LTB4, new in 1928, pictured below on the Llanberis excursion in 1933. While the passengers enjoy a photo break the driver, Edgar Jenkinson, sits immediately behind the offside front wheel. (BSC)

The wide range of destinations available is evident from this 1930 advert in the Rochdale Observer for the annual Wakes Holidays. Even in those days you could get to Scarborough, Llangollen, Llandudno, York, Bridlington and Windermere, and even as far as Stratford-upon-Avon and Gretna Green. You could also get half day trips to more local destinations such as Blackpool and Southport, or Manchester's Belle Vue Pleasure Grounds.

An occasional destination for a day out was Wembley Stadium on the occasion of a big football match or, more importantly to Rochdale, the Rugby League Cup Final. In the upper view GDK 122, one of the two 1948 Leyland PS1/1 Tigers rebuilt with a full-fronted Burlingham Seagull body in 1955, arrives at the Empire Stadium with a load of supporters. *(EOC)*

In the lower photograph it is the turn of SDK 442, the second of the Plaxton-bodied Leyland Worldmasters, to make the trip. *(EOC)*

The imaginative excursion to London Airport in 1967. Eric Smith is driving HDK 751E with Alan Schofield as co-driver. In this busy traffic scene within the airport's boundary the bonnet of a Triumph Herald can be seen in the bottom left of the picture, while to the right is a rare Humber Super Snipe estate car. The coach is seen when new, before rebodying in 1975. *(BSC)*

HDK 751E on a Yorkshire Dales excursion pauses for a coffee break at Skipton. (*EOC both*)

Former Leyland demonstrator, Royal Tiger Doyen D387 VAO, on a holiday tour at Torquay in 1991.

Ellen Smith provided the team coaches for both Rochdale Hornets Rugby League Club and Rochdale Football Club. Douglas Neal was photographed above with ODK 137 for an article in the Rochdale Observer on how the teams travelled around the country. Harry Smith kept these pictures on his desk at the Wardleworth office for many years. *(BSC)*

On the opposite page is Douglas Neal's work ticket for a Rochdale Hornets Rugby League match at Workington on 31st March 1973. Lunch and dinner stops are specified. *(DN)*

Form 1 (upper)

ROAD TRAFFIC ACT 1934 SECTION 25

WORK TICKET & RECORD

COMPILED IN ACCORDANCE WITH
THE PUBLIC VEHICLES (CONTRACT
CARRIAGE RECORDS) REGULATIONS
1961

PART 1

NAME & ADDRESS OF P.S.V. LICENCE HOLDER: MARDLEWORTH GARAGE

ROCHDALE

REGISTRATION MARK OF VEHICLE: TDK594J

NAME(S) OF DRIVER(S): D. NEAL

NAME AND FULL ADDRESS OF ORGANISER(B): Rochdale Metro W.E. Block

Rochdale

PART 2 — PARTICULARS OF JOURNEY

	COL. 1 PROPOSED	COL. 2 ACTUAL (if Different from proposed) (C)
STARTING PLACE	GROUND, THEN NEWGATE	
DATE	VFT. 31/03/73	
TIME	9.15	A.M./P.M.
DESTINATION	WORKINGTON	
DATE		
TIME		A.M./P.M.
ROUTE	River Forton	
	River Brown	
	Eamont Bridge	
MILEAGE	Tackley	A.M./P.M.

PART 3

(THIS PART TO BE SIGNED WITHIN 72 HOURS OF THE JOURNEY)
THE JOURNEY WAS MADE AS SHOWN IN COLUMN 1 OF PART 2 ABOVE

SUBJECT TO ALTERATIONS SHOWN IN COLUMN 2 OF THAT PART.

SIGNATURE OF HOLDER OF P.S.V. LICENCE OR PERSON AUTHORISED BY HIM TO SIGN:-

DATE OF SIGNATURE: 31/3/73

SIGNATURE OF DRIVER

Kalamazoo 227738-85

Form 2 (lower)

ROAD TRAFFIC ACT 1934 SECTION 25

WORK TICKET & RECORD

COMPILED IN ACCORDANCE WITH
THE PUBLIC VEHICLES (CONTRACT
CARRIAGE RECORDS) REGULATIONS
1961

PART 1

NAME & ADDRESS OF P.S.V. LICENCE HOLDER: MARDLEWORTH GARAGE

ROCHDALE

REGISTRATION MARK OF VEHICLE: TDK594J

NAME(S) OF DRIVER(S): D. NEAL

NAME AND FULL ADDRESS OF ORGANISER(B): Allo Pat Mull

Littleboro' Disabled Club

PART 2 — PARTICULARS OF JOURNEY

	COL. 1 PROPOSED	COL. 2 ACTUAL (if Different from proposed) (C)
STARTING PLACE	DISABLED CLUB, LITTLEBOROUGH	
DATE	VFT. 10/12/75	
TIME	9.45	A.M./P.M.
DESTINATION	LITTLEBOROUGH & SUBURBS	
	& IND GARAGE	
DATE		
TIME		A.M./P.M.
ROUTE		
MILEAGE		

PART 3

(THIS PART TO BE SIGNED WITHIN 72 HOURS OF THE JOURNEY)
THE JOURNEY WAS MADE AS SHOWN IN COLUMN 1 OF PART 2 ABOVE

SUBJECT TO ALTERATIONS SHOWN IN COLUMN 2 OF THAT PART.

SIGNATURE OF HOLDER OF P.S.V. LICENCE OR PERSON AUTHORISED BY HIM TO SIGN:-

DATE OF SIGNATURE: 10 12 15

SIGNATURE OF DRIVER

Kalamazoo 227738-85

59

A large crowd can be seen gathered outside the the old booking office in Newgate around 1971. The buildings in the middle background have long been demolished to make way for the Exchange shopping centre. Work is progressing on the Lonsdale House office block on the left. (DNC)

At the same spot Rochdale Hornets' Rugby League team coach NDK 18G waits at the left while supporters gather round PDK 763H prior to travelling to the away match. In this group is Hornets' Secretary Fred Kershaw (with sideburns and cap). *(DNC)*

Summer 1934 and the passengers on a tour of the Lake District stand in the afternoon sunshine at the top of the Kirkstone Pass while Burlingham-bodied Leyland Tiger DK 9092 cools down after the long climb up from Ullswater. (*EOC*)

Edinburgh was always a popular tour destination. A886 OND is pictured in the Scottish capital in November 1986, showing part of the city's famous skyline with Calton Hill and the North British Hotel in the background. (EO)

Douglas Neal and ODK 137 ponder the best route to Rothesay at this road sign at the north end of the Isle of Bute in spring 1969. Eventually they arrive in Rothesay only to find a Scotch mist. *(DN both)*

Douglas Neal with ODK 137 outside he hotel at Rothesay on the Isle of the Bute.

Douglas Neal again with ODK 137, parked up at the Forth railway bridge in August 1969. *(DN both)*

The other end of the country. ODK 137 at Lands End, Cornwall in the summer of 1969. *(DN)*

SDK 442 stands in the picturesque village of Lower Slaughter in May 1966 while on a tour of the Cotswolds. *(BSC)*

What the passenger doesn't see. Eric Smith cleans the coach late at night after returning from an excursion to London in 1967. All exterior cleaning was by bucket and brush since planning could not be obtained for a vehicle wash because of the risk of polluting the Hey Brook alongside the garage. *(BSC)*

This later view shows the then new booking office on the Town Hall Square in 1974, the side of the Town Hall being behind the camera. Waiting outside the office, these coaches are loading for holidays at Scarborough, Rhyl, Southport and Bridlington, and will bring the holidaymakers home the following Saturday. (BSC)

In this second photograph 6733 DK, driven by Douglas Harper, has pulled out on its way to Southport, leaving the other three coaches still loading the holidaymakers with their suitcases. *(BSC)*

Staff

Harry Smith was astute in his choice of drivers. He looked for men skilled in various trades who not only held PSV licences but could also turn their hand to in-house maintenance work on both the vehicles and the building. For example, Clifford Howard and Peter Tod were trained mechanics, Alan Schofield was a joiner, Derek Johnson was a tyre fitter and Jack Mills could paint professionally. Douglas Harper, a part-time driver during the 1950s, '60s and '70s, later became a full-time mechanic.

Douglas Neal, who trained as an auto-electrician, came to Ellen Smith in 1965 as a driver and a mechanic. He stayed until after the sale to Rossendale in 1991, though with spells away as a tour driver with Glenton Tours of London and Wallace Arnold in Devon. On joining Rossendale he was appointed coaching manager until he resigned later that year. Alan Schofield started in 1965 and drove throughout with the Smiths and continues today as a driver in Paul Targett's operation.

Being specialists in other trades guaranteed work all year round, especially on maintenance and preparing coaches for the main season from Easter until the end of the Blackpool Illuminations. There was, of course, driving work out of season on private hire and away football and rugby matches.

The doyen of the staff was undoubtedly Ken Barker, the chief engineer, who started with Ellen Smith after the war and stayed until the sale of the company when he retired having attained 45 years service. Ken could turn his hand to anything mechanical. Long before Range Rover announced a diesel version, Ken fitted a J- registered example with a Perkins 3-litre diesel engine from an old refuse vehicle. In his earlier years he had been a keen motor cyclist and once won a local rally on a vintage 1921 Triumph 550 side-valve.

Ken, who served in both the Merchant Navy and the Royal Navy during the war, is a powerful man over 6 f. tall, who could lift two road springs, oxygen bottles and 56 lb weights with ease. He could reline front brakes in 20 minutes and change a road spring in two hours. Ken was expert at fault-finding on engines using his stethoscope. He once received a written commendation from Scania for finding an elusive fault on an engine in a truck belonging to 'young' Edgar Jenkinson. He diagnosed the problem but the Scania engineers were sceptical. The engine was stripped down and the fault discovered exactly as Ken had stated.

Ken was a genius at tuning engines. An Ellen Smith coach was seen to have overtaken a specially built Midland Red motorway coach before the speed limits were introduced on the motorways. Reports of this incident found their way to Leyland and two Leyland engineers appeared at the garage requesting to inspect the coach involved. Impressed with what they saw and with Ken's advice on Leyland engines, he was invited to work for Leyland but he decided to stay with Ellen Smith. The company had a reputation among drivers as being among the fastest on the road, all due to Ken's tuning.

At one time Ken lived on a farm on the moors above Wardle and always brought a pint of milk to work each day. On arrival at the garage entrance, he would let out a shout of 'YOU' in true military fashion and throw a bottle at the nearest person. His colleagues became proficient in fielding the flying milk bottle and very rarely missed a catch!

Douglas Neal tells of his experience when taking Rochdale Youth Band to London for the School Band semi-finals in July 1971. There was a mix-up between the Cromwell Road hotels booked for the party which meant that there was no accommodation for him. Douglas decided he would drive to St Margaret's near Richmond and stay with his aunt and uncle who lived there. Cyril Smith, the MP for Rochdale, was attending the event, learned of Douglas's predicament and promptly gave him the key to his room. Douglas asked the MP where he was going to sleep. "Not my problem." said Cyril. "The hotel will have to come up with something or there will be trouble." Needless to say, they did.

Many coach drivers have their eccentricities. Among Ellen Smith drivers were Bob Hollis and Roy Milne. Bob liked to clean up the white lines outside the garage in Yorkshire Street. He also possessed the doubtful attribute of the ability to walk on his hands. He had a habit of circling Marjorie while doing so, much to her discomfiture. Marjorie once caught Roy spraying her cats with a hose pipe which resulted in four weeks of the worst kind of jobs being allocated to him. One of Marjorie's cats, a black one called Snowy, could usually be seen sitting on top of the photo copier in the office.

Eric Smith as a boy with a friend sitting on the bumper of DK 5053, the 1928 Burlingham-bodied Leyland Lioness LTB4 charabanc. The picture is taken near Llanberis circa 1933. *(BSC)*

Above:
Driver Edgar Jenkinson with Lioness DK 5053, circa 1933. *(BSC)*

Right:
Eric Smith and Alan Schofield seen aboard HDK 751E at London Airport in 1967. *(LJ)*

From 1977, Douglas Neal worked for a period with Glenton Tours of London, a high class operator specialising in servicing American tourists visiting Britain. Setting out on a holiday to John O' Groats in August 1981, he discovered that the oil filter was faulty. He rang Harry Smith from Dunstable and arranged to drop off his passengers at Newgate in Rochdale (where they could experience a typical Lancashire town as part of their overall view of Britain) and drive to the Wardleworth garage. Here, Ken Barker and Douglas Harper exchanged the faulty filter for a new one from Ellen Smith stock. With no charge for the repair, the arrangement was that Douglas Neal would bring a new filter the next time he passed through the town, which he did. This story illustrates the goodwill which exists between most coach operators. The picture shows Harry Smith inspecting the Glenton Plaxton-bodied Leopard PYT 155R. Ellen Smith's Duple-bodied Leopard PDK 829M is at the left. *(DN)*

Examples of Harry Smith's signwriting are seen here when Douglas Neal visited the garage with his Glenton coach. Note the prices for the Fylde Coast in the summer of 1981. In this picture Harry Smith walks across the entrance while Bill Neal (Douglas's father), Derek Johnson and a local plumber look on. *(DN)*

Four Ellen Smith drivers at London's Vauxhall Bridge coach park in September 1967. From left to right Douglas Harper, Donny Bamford, Derek Johnson and Douglas Neal. *(DN)*

A series of Lancashire Coach Drivers' cabaret evenings were held in the late 1960s and early 1970s. The idea came about as the result of an invitation from Stanley Gath of Dewsbury to attend a coach drivers' social evening at a club in Royston near Barnsley in 1966. The first one was held at Whitworth Civic Hall and later ones at Heywood Civic Hall. The events proved successful with coaches from Lancashire, Yorkshire and Cheshire parked all round the Civic Hall. Among a group at Heywood are: Front row 4th Alan Schofield; 6th Douglas Neal; 7th Beryl Mills (wife of Jack, sister of Betty Smith). Back row 3rd left Ken Barker; 4th Cliff Howard; 5th Roy Bamford; 6th Eric Smith. The year is thought to be 1971. *(DN)*

A reunion of some former Ellen Smith staff on 12th March 2009. From left to right Douglas Harper, Derek Johnson (standing), Ken Barker, Douglas Neal, Eric Ogden (author), Alan Schofield (standing) and Paul Targett (Director of the present Ellen Smith (Tours) Ltd.) *(NO)*

YDK 869 and 'Young' Edgar Jenkinson competing in the National Coach Rally at Blackpool. This coach had a dramatic life. During summer 1966 it was involved in a serious road traffic accident at Frodsham on an excursion to Llandudno. It ran into stationary traffic when rammed in the rear by an HGV. This resulted in the front being badly damaged, both windscreen glasses smashed and the rear was badly impacted, the rear bench seat being forced forward into the rearmost pair of seats. It received major repairs at Plaxton in Scarborough since Harrington had closed down the previous year, being driven overnight by Douglas Neal with fleet engineer Ken Barker following in his Land Rover. As the fleet was then minus a coach for the rest of the summer, a Harrington-bodied AEC Reliance, 449 GYV, was hired in for several months from Fallowfield & Britten Ltd of London N16, a member of the George Ewer Group. Unfortunately, no photograph of this coach has been found. It was driven mainly by Jack Cavanagh, known as 'Cracker Jack.' Despite its success in the 1961 Rally, YDK 869 was regarded as a 'jinx' coach as it was involved in another serious accident on the North Yorkshire Moors. It was repaired and refurbished in the garage by Ellen Smith staff and carried from then on a set of Plaxton seats. On withdrawal in 1976 it passed to a local operator for further service. *(BSC)*

CDK 448C at the back of the Wardleworth workshops and below resplendent in the sunshine in the garage yard. (*EOC both*)

A distant view of the garage from the Lancashire and Yorkshire Railway bridge over Yorkshire Street. Taken c1955 the picture shows the full-fronted Harrington bodied Leyland Tiger HDK 812 of 1951 parked at the side of the garage. The rare Austin Sheerline car parked opposite the garage was owned by one of the drivers. (EOC)

This later picture, taken in 1970, was commissioned by Harry Smith on delivery of his new coach PDK 763H with Harry at the wheel. It was taken from the far side of the bridge, which carried the Rochdale to Bacup branch line. The branch is long closed and the bridge demolished, but the building to the right and Heybrook School still stand. Prominent in both pictures are now politically incorrect advertisements for cigarettes. *(DNC)*

D892 PNB, a 1986 Leyland Royal Tiger Doyen, entered the fleet on 1st January 1987 and was the star of the Leyland stand at the Coach and Bus Show held in the National Exhibition Centre, Birmingham in October 1986. It is pictured here surrounded by visitors to the show. *(JJH)*

This picture epitomises the rapid development in coach bodies in the immediate post-war period. These two Leyland Tigers were virtually identical mechanically, but look very different. HDK 236 on the left, with a traditional half-cab, was new in 1950, while GDK 122 on the right was actually two years older, but its original body was replaced by a new Burlingham Seagull full-fronted body in 1955. *(EOC)*

This is the only photograph that has been found of LDK 445, a 1954 AEC Regal IV with Harrington body. It was a departure from the fleet standard and remained in the fleet for only eleven years. *(EOC)*

Two views of RDK 4, the 1957 Leyland Tiger Cub with Duple body, photographed on the Blackpool coach park. *(EO)*

SDK 442 was the second of Ellen Smith's two Leyland Royal Tiger Worldmasters. Originally carrying a Plaxton C41C body, it was rebodied by Plaxton in 1970 as shown in the upper picture, at Middle Walk Blackpool on a Ribble Enthusiasts Club Southport to Blackpool Event and again in preservation in the lower picture. *(NO; EOC)*

Two views of XDK 279, Ellen Smith's first Leyland L1T with Harrington body. New in 1960 Eric Smith drove this coach from then until taking over HDK 751E in 1967. *(DN)*

Offside and nearside views of 3161 DK, Ellen Smith's first coach built to the newly permitted maximum length of 36ft in 1962. This followed the revision of the Construction and Use regulations and allowed an increase in seating from 41 to 51, which had a significant effect on the economics of the business. The upper view shows 3161 DK in Rawtenstall opposite the cricket ground on Bacup Road. *(EOC)*

During Wakes Week holidays it was common practice for coach operators to sub-contract to one another to cover the resulting peaks in traffic. CDK 448C is pictured here in that capacity on hire to Robinson's of Great Harwood. *(EOC)*

After the company's previous success in the Brighton Rally it entered FDK 94D, a brand new Plaxton-bodied Leopard, in the 1966 event. Unsuccessful there, it later won the Paignton Hotel Association Cup. After 19 years service it was sold to a jazz band in Hyde. *(EOC both)*

HDK 119E was one of two Plaxton-bodied Bedford VAM14s, new in 1967, which replaced the Bedford SB5s acquired with the business of Benjamin Barnes of Rawtenstall some three years earlier. They remained in the fleet until 1972. *(DNC)*

CDK 373L was a 12-metre Leopard with a Plaxton body which joined the fleet in 1973 and is seen here on an excursion to Fleetwood in May 1989. *(NO)*

PDK 763H, the 1970 Leyland Leopard wth Plaxton C49F body. *(EOC)*

Duple-bodied Leopard PDK 829M dating from 1974. This was the last Ellen Smith coach to carry the local DK registration letters. *(EO)*

Three Ellen Smith coaches, LCB 652P, CFS 264S and YDK 165L at the Oldham Athletic football ground at Boundary Park, ready to take fans to an away match. *(EO)*

FTD 758W, the Duple Dominant-bodied Leyland Tiger, is seen at Halifax on a misty day in September 1981. *(EO)*

PDK 829M was the Leyland Leopard with a Duple body purchased in 1974. It is seen here in the later livery after re-panelling which makes an interesting comparison with the picture on page 39. *(EOC)*

1984 Plaxton-bodied Leyland Tiger A886 OND was the first coach in the fleet to carry a new year-prefix registration. *(EO)*

A sad sight as the once luxurious Harrington Cavalier moulders away behind the garage in 1981. New in 1963 4728 DK gave 15 years service before being put out to grass. In 1985 it was removed by a dealer for scrapping along with UDK 551, seen in the background with its Maidstone and District front and Tiger Cub RDK 4, just visible through the cab of the Cavalier.. *(EO)*

All In A Coach Driver's Life

An extract from Douglas Neal's diary covering two weeks in June 1972 driving Leyland Leopard TDK 594J. This was, of course, before the current stringent drivers' hours regulations which restrict not only daily driving hours but many once popular tour periods.

18th Sun	Half day excursion to Stratford on Avon.
19th Mon	Full day excursion to London (with 2nd man).
20th Tue	Full day excursion to Morecambe.
21st Wed	Full day excursion to Weston super Mare (with 2nd man).
22nd Thu	Full day excursion to Morecambe.
23rd Fri	Full day excursion to Bourton on the Water (with 2nd man).
24th Sat	Southport with long date holiday passengers.
25th Sun	Full day excursion to Southend (with 2nd man).
26th Mon	Full day excursion to Pontefract races.
27th Tue	Full day excursion to Woburn Safari Park.
28th Wed	Full day excursion to Edinburgh (with 2nd man).
29th Thu	Full day excursion to Yorkshire Dales.
30th Fri	Torquay overnight with long date holiday passengers.
1st July Sat	Return from Torquay.
2nd Sun	Half day excursion to Gretna Green.

An imaginative programme indeed but hard and concentrated work for the driver. However, professional coach drivers are a special breed with a special aptitude and enjoy their work.

A coach driver has to be prepared for anything, and not just on the road. Douglas Neal drove a tour to Torquay in TDK 594J for the Rochdale Blind Welfare in October 1972. During the evening one of the passengers was found dead in the toilet having suffered a heart attack. The following day on an excursion to Teignmouth another passenger collapsed with a heart attack and Douglas had to call and rendezvous with an ambulance. The passenger was released from Exeter Hospital four days later but was only allowed to travel home by car. Douglas arranged for the Rochdale Hospital's contractor to bring his car to Torquay, stay overnight at the hotel and drive the patient home the next day.

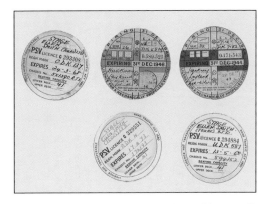

Various licence discs. Long-time drivers will remember the style of the 1944 and 1946 discs. DK 7182 was a 1931 Leyland Tiger TS1 with Burlingham 32-seat body withdrawn in 1950, and DK 5819 was a 1929 Leyland LTB1 Lioness with Lewis & Crabtree dual-door 26-seat coachwork withdrawn in 1951. *(JM to DN)*

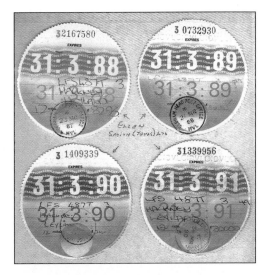

Licence discs for LFS 487T for the years to 31st March 1988, 1989, 1990 and 1991. *(DN)*

Year	Registration	Chassis type	Body type	and seating	Withd'n	Disposal	Notes
1915	DK 594	Belsize	Lorry/Chara	CH	?	unknown	New 1919 - ex War Dept Chassis converted 1919
1920	FY 2331	Karrier WDS	Lorry/Chara	CH	?	unknown	
1920	TB 2788	Daimler CK	Lorry/Chara	CH	?	unknown	
1921	CW 2009	Maudslay C5	Lorry/Chara	CH34	1925	Allen, Stalybridge (Lorry) 1926	New 1919
1922	FY 4140	Leyland M	-?-	CH28	1934	Morris, Newton Heath (Lorry) 1934	New 1921 toThompson &Culshaw Southport
1924	TC 7987	Leyland	-?-	CH	?	unknown	
1925	TD 2333	Albion PF24	Burlingham	CH18	by 1935	Kenyon, Manchester (Lorry) by1935	
1926	TD 6328	Albion PFA26	Burlingham	C20D	by 1934	unidentified, St Helens 1934	
1927	DK 4081	Leyland PLC1	J Crabtree ?	C26F	1937	Lytham St Annes 22; rebodied Burlingham OB31R	
1927	DK 4393	Albion PFB26	Cowieson	C23R	1931	T Barnes, Oldham (Lorry) 1931	
1928	DK 5053	Leyland PLC1	Burlingham	C26D	1937	Lytham St Annes 23; rebodied Burlingham OB31R	To Ministry of Supply 1941
1929	DK 5819	Leyland Lioness LTB1	Lewis & Crabtree	C26D	1951	Aitken & Son, Edenfield	To Ministry of Supply 1941
1929	DK 5915	Leyland Lioness LTB1	Fielden & Bottomley	C26D	1951	scrapped 1953	later reseated to C27F
1930	DK 6440	Leyland Lioness LTB1	Burlingham	C26D	1951	Aitken & Son, Edenfield by 1955	later reseated to C27F
1931	DK 7182	Leyland Tiger TS1	Burlingham	C32R	1950	Edco Fabrics, Burnley, 1950 as a Staff Bus	later reseated to C27F; also quoted as Shearing
1932	DK 7757	Leyland Tiger TS4	Harrington	C32R	1951	C & H, Fleetwood 1951 as C33F	Rebodied Shearing & Crabtree
1932	DK 7758	Leyland Tiger TS4	Harrington	C32R	1951	Johnston Bros, Litherland 1952 as C33F	Rebodied Shearing & Crabtree
1933	DK 8356	Leyland Tiger TS4 Diesel	Roberts	C32R	1956	War Dept 1940-46; Sutcliffe, Todmorden 1956	Rebodied Challenger C33F 1947 (assemb'd at garage)
1934	DK 9092	Leyland Tiger TS6	Burlingham	C32R	1957	Banfield, London by1960	Rebodied Challenger C33F 1947
1935	DK 9883	Leyland Tiger TS6 Petrol	Burlingham	C32R	1940	War Dept 1940: Air Ministry 1941	later reseated to C33F
1936	ADK 989	Leyland Tiger TS7 Petrol	Harrington	C32F	1956	not traced further – presumed scrapped	
1947	FDK 731	Leyland Tiger PS1/1	Plaxton	C33F	1957	Banfield, London by1960	Rebodied Burlingham FC33F 1955
1948	GDK 121	Leyland Tiger PS1/1	Challenger	C33F	1964	Cowley (dealer), Salford, then to Doric Unit Co, Lumb-in-Rossendale 1964 (staff bus)	Rebodied Burlingham FC33F 1955
1948	GDK 122	Leyland Tiger PS1/1	Challenger	C33F	1964	Shamrock Bus Service, Thurles, Tipperary 1964	
1950	HDK 80	Daimler CVD6	Burlingham	C35F	1961	Johnson, Wyke, Bradford 1961	
1950	HDK 236	Leyland Tiger PS2/3	Burlingham	C33F	1964	Scully, Mountmellick, Eire 1964	
1951	HDK 812	Leyland Tiger PS2/3	Harrington	FC35F	1965	John Warburton Ltd, Haslingden 1965 (non PSV)	
1952	JDK 412	Leyland Royal Tiger PSU1/15	Harrington	C41C	1965	not traced - presumed scrapped c1966	
1953	KDK 1	Leyland Royal Tiger PSU1/16	Harrington	C41C	1965	not traced - presumed scrapped c1966	
1954	LDK 445	AEC Regal IV	Harrington	C41C	1965	not traced - presumed scrapped c1966	
1956	ODK 137	Leyland Worldmaster RT3/1	Plaxton	C41C	1979	Robinson, Bolton	Rebodied Plaxton C43F 1968
1957	RDK 4	Leyland Tiger Cub PSUC1/2	Duple	C41C	1974	Lister (dealer), Bolton 1985	
1958	SDK 442	Leyland Worldmaster RT3/2	Plaxton	C41C	1983	Bolton Transport Group 1983 (on loan)	Rebodied Plaxton C41F 1970
1959	UDK 551	Leyland Tiger Cub PSUC1/2	Harrington	C41F	1974	Lister (dealer), Bolton 1985	
1960	XDK 279	Leyland Leopard L1T	Harrington	C41F	1977	279 Preservation Group, Liversedge 1977	
1961	YDK 869	Leyland Leopard L2T	Harrington	C41F	1976	King, Rochdale 1976	
1962	3017 DK	Bedford SB5	Harrington	C41F	1966	Durie & Miller, Haslingden by1969 (staff bus)	
1962	3161 DK	Leyland Leopard PSU3/3RT	Harrington	C51F	1975	Pearson, Heywood 1975	
1963	4728 DK	Leyland Leopard PSU3/3RT	Harrington	C45F	1978	Lister (dealer), Bolton 1985	
1963	6733 DK	Leyland Leopard PSU3/3RT	Harrington	C49F	1979	Dean (Classique Sun Saloon Coaches), Paisley 1979	To Preservation 1991 as EDS 584B
1964	539 XTF	Bedford SB5	Duple	C41F	1967	Lloyd, Shouldham 1967	
1964	540 XTF	Bedford SB5	Duple	C41F	1967	Tucker, Melsham 1967	Ex B Barnes, Rawtenstall (new 1962)
1965	CDK 448C	Leyland Leopard PSU3/3RT	Harrington	C49F	1986	Rothwell, Heywood 1991 (preserved)	Ex B Barnes, Rawtenstall (new 1962)
1966	FDK 94D	Leyland Leopard PSU3/3RT	Plaxton	C49F	1985	Zodiac Jazz Band, Hyde	
1966	FDK 187D	AEC Reliance	Plaxton	C41F	1986	Stock Car Transporter, Rochdale	Refurbished 1984
1967	HDK 118E	Bedford VAM14	Plaxton	C45F	1972	Moxon, Oldcotes 1973	

Year	Reg.	Chassis type	Body	Seating	Year	Disposal	Notes
1967	HDK 119E	Bedford VAM14	Plaxton	C45F	1972	Moxon, Oldcotes 1973	Rebodied Plaxton C51F 1975
1967	HDK 751E	Leyland Leopard PSU3/4RT	Plaxton	C49F	1988	Robinson, Bolton 1989	
1969	NDK 18G	Leyland Leopard PSU4/4RT	Plaxton	C43F	1988	Terrington, Oldham 1988 (preserved / caravan)	
1970	PDK 763H	Leyland Leopard PSU3A/4RT	Plaxton	C49F	1986	mobile caravan by1992	
1971	TDK 594J	Leyland Leopard PSU3B/4RT	Plaxton	C51F	1986	Booth (D & M Coaches), Blackpool 1986	
1972	WDK 916K	Leyland Leopard PSU3B/4RT	Plaxton	C51F	1986	Holt Drive, Bolton 1989	
1972	YDK 165L	Leyland Leopard PSU5/4RT	Plaxton	C57F	1991	Rossendale Transport 314 28/1/91	
1973	CDK 373L	Leyland Leopard PSU5/4RT	Plaxton	C57F	1990	Chartercoach, Great Oakley 1990	
1974	PDK 829M	Leyland Leopard PSU5/4R	Duple	C57F	1991	Rossendale Transport 313 28/1/91	
1975	HTD 589N	Leyland Leopard PSU5A/4RT	Plaxton	C57F	1991	Rossendale Transport 312 28/1/91	Refurbished 1986
1976	LCB 652P	Leyland Leopard PSU5A/4RT	Plaxton	C57F	1991	Rossendale Transport 311 28/1/91	
1977	UGG 369R	Leyland Leopard PSU3C/4R	Plaxton	C53F	1991	Rossendale Transport 310 28/1/91	Reseated to C49F
1978	CFS 264S	Leyland Leopard PSU5B/4R	Plaxton	C53F	1991	Rossendale Transport 309 28/1/91	
1979	LFS 487T	Leyland Leopard PSU3E/4R	Plaxton	C49F	1991	Rossendale Transport 308 28/1/91	
1980	UFS 690V	Leyland Leopard PSU5C/5R	Plaxton	C53F	1991	Rossendale Transport 307 28/1/91	
1981	FTD 758W	Leyland Tiger TRCTL11/3R	Duple	C53F	1991	Rossendale Transport 306 28/1/91	
1983	FJA 400Y	Leyland Tiger TRCTL11/3R	Plaxton	C53F	1991	Rossendale Transport 305 28/1/91	
1984	A886 OND	Leyland Tiger TRCTL11/3R	Plaxton	C53F	1991	Rossendale Transport 304 28/1/91	
1984	B887 WRJ	Leyland Tiger TRCTL11/3RZ	Plaxton	C53F	1991	Rossendale Transport 303 28/1/91	
1987	D892 PNB	Leyland Royal Tiger RTC	Leyland	C53F	1991	Rossendale Transport 301 28/1/91	
1988	D387 VAO	Leyland Royal Tiger RTC	Leyland	C53F	1991	Rossendale Transport 302 28/1/91	ex Leyland Demonstrator. New in 1987 as C49FT

The following Ellen Smith vehicles are believed to still be in current preservation:

SDK 442 – Museum of Transport, M/c   6733 DK – now registered EDS 584B and with Norman, Hull   CDK 448C – Rogers, Kidderminster

XDK 279 sold initially into preservation, ended its days as a Stock Car Transporter   NDK 18G was sold out of preservation by1989.

Further details on the vehicles taken over by Rossendale Transport, including details of their new registration numbers appear in the next section.

ROSSENDALE TRANSPORT LIMITED

Former Ellen Smith vehicles acquired by Rossendale Transport Limited – 28th January 1991

No.	Original Reg.	New Reg.	Chassis type	Body type and seating	New	Date Out	Disposal
301	D892 PNB	OIB 5401	Leyland Royal Tiger RTC	Leyland Doyen C53F	1987	1993	Stephenson, Rochford
302	D387 VAO	OIB 5402	Leyland Royal Tiger RTC	Leyland Doyen C53F	1987	1993	Stephenson, Rochford
303	B887 WRJ	OIB 5403	Leyland Tiger TRCTL11/3RZ	Plaxton Paramount 3200 C53F	1985	2002	Ripley (dealer), Carlton
304	A886 OND	OIB 3604	Leyland Tiger TRCTL11/3R	Plaxton Paramount 3200 C53F	1984	1999	Reddin, Muff, Ireland
305	FJA 400Y	OIB 6205	Leyland Tiger TRCTL11/3R	Plaxton Paramount 3200 C53F	1983	1999	Owls Coaches, Long Ditton
306	FTD 758W	OIB 8606	Leyland Tiger TRCTL11/3R	Duple Dominant IVC53F	1981	1994	Timeline Travel 24
307	UFS 690V	OIB 6207	Leyland Leopard PSU5C/5R	Plaxton Supreme C53F	1980	1996	Border Tours, Burnley 307
308	LFS 487T	OIB 3608	Leyland Leopard PSU3E/4R	Plaxton Supreme C49F	1979	1996	Border Tours, Burnley 308
309	CFS 264S		Leyland Leopard PSU5B/4R	Plaxton Supreme C53F	1978	1994	Border Tours, Burnley 309
310	UGG 369R	see notes	Leyland Leopard PSU3C/4R	Plaxton Supreme C49F	1977	1992	Rossendale 77 (rebodied)
311	LCB 652P		Leyland Leopard PSU5A/4R	Plaxton Supreme C57F	1976	1993	Border Tours, Burnley 311
312	HTD 589N		Leyland Leopard PSU5A/4R	Plaxton Panorama Elite III C57F	1975	1994	Ripley (dealer), Carlton
313	PDK 829M		Leyland Leopard PSU5/4R	Duple Dominant C57F	1974	1991	Border Tours, Burnley 413
314	YDK 165L		Leyland Leopard PSU5/4R	Plaxton Panorama Elite II C57F	1972	1991	Border Tours, Burnley 414

Notes

All vehicles were purchased new by Ellen Smith, except for 302 which was a former Leyland demonstrator, purchased by Ellen Smith in 1988 and operated in its demonstration colour scheme.

The re-registrations into the 'OIB' series all took place during June and August 1991, except for 301, which didn't receive OIB 5401 until July 1993.

Vehicles sold to Border Tours had been on loan at various intervals prior to being officially sold to them.

304/5 are believed to have been sold to a dealer prior to passing to their respective new operators.

310 received a new East Lancs B51F body in December 1992 for use in the Rossendale bus fleet and was re-registered PJI 9177 in June 1993.

311 was to have been re-registered TXI 5511, but this never took place.

312 went on loan to Border Tours, Burnley from September 1992 to August 1993 and was then exchanged for 311. It was renumbered 412 in 1993, but this fleetnumber was never carried on the vehicle.

314 was renumbered 414 in March 1991.

A separate subsidiary company of Rossendale Transport, Tripvast Limited was formed in November 1990 to acquire the various assets that would comprise the deal. Tripvast Limited was then renamed to Ellen Smith (Tours) Limited on the 1st April 1991.

All the acquired vehicles operated on the Rossendale Transport Operator Licence (PC1838) until 1996, when a separate Operator Licence in the name of Ellen Smith (Tours) Limited was granted (PC4092). Prior to this, the Ellen Smith subsidiary progressively absorbed many vehicles of the Rossendale Coach Hire fleet, details of which are listed below.

ROSSENDALE TRANSPORT LIMITED

Former Rossendale Transport vehicles transferred to the Ellen Smith Subsidiary (from 1991)

No.	Original Reg.	New Reg.	Chassis type	Body type and seating	New	Date In	Date Out	Former Operator
80	B66 YFV	LIB 1180	Leyland Tiger TRCTL11/3RZ	Plaxton Paramount 3500 C49FT	1985	1992	1996	Ribble 1006
85	A110 EPA	OIB 1285	Leyland Tiger TRCTL11/2RH	Plaxton Paramount 3200 C53F	1983	1991	1993	Kentish Bus 4
86		DKG 272V	Leyland Leopard PSU3F/5R	Plaxton Supreme IV C53F	1980	1991	1992	Hill, Tredegar
88	D888 YHG	HIL 3188	Leyland Olympian ONTL11/2RH	East Lancs CH47/31F	1987	1992	1994	new
370	NIW 6515	170 BHR	Volvo B10M-61	Van Hool C49FT	1981	1993	1995	Hardman, Waterfoot
381	GBO 243W	LIB 1181	Leyland Leopard PSU3F/5R	Plaxton Supreme IV C53F	1980	1993	1996	Hill, Tredegar
383	NDW 149X	LIB 1183	Leyland Tiger TRCTL11/2R	Plaxton Supreme VI C53F	1982	1994	1998	Hill, Tredegar
384	NDW 148X	LIB 1184	Leyland Tiger TRCTL11/2R	Plaxton Supreme VI C53F	1982	1994	1998	Hill, Tredegar
387	A133 EPA	OIB 1287	Leyland Tiger TRCTL11/2RH	Plaxton Paramount 3200 C53F	1984	1995	1999	Kentish Bus 7
389	A148 EPA	LIW 4289	Leyland Tiger TRCTL11/3R	Plaxton Paramount 3200C51F	1984	1990	1999	Kentish Bus 103
390		D741 ALR	MCW Metrorider MF150/6	MCW C20F	1987	1991	1999	Capital, West Drayton

Notes

80 repainted into Ellen Smith 'traditional' style livery in March 1992 and renumbered 380 circa April 1993.

85 retained its 'Rossendale Coach Hire' livery and was allocated fleetnumber 385, but this was not carried on the vehicle.

86 was renumbered 386 in March 1991 and retained 'Rossendale Coach Hire' livery.

88 was allocated fleetnumber 388 during its stay in the Ellen Smith fleet, but this was never carried on the vehicle.

370 was previously registered 942 AYA and was new as STT 604X.

381 retained 'Rossendale Coach Hire' livery and its Rossendale Operator Licence.

383/4/7/9 were all repainted into Ellen Smith 'traditional' style livery (ex Rossendale Coach Hire).

390 was painted in 'traditional' style Ellen Smith livery and was re-registered 170 BHR in March 1995. Allocated to the Whiteways operation in 1996 and repainted into the mainly red 'Grand Luxe' livery.

Fleet Additions by Rossendale Transport Limited for the Ellen Smith fleet

No.	Original Reg.	New Reg.	Chassis type	Body type and seating	New	Date In	Date Out	Former Operator
314	KAD 356V	NIW 6514	Leyland Leopard PSU5C/4R	Plaxton C53F	1980	1991	1996	Parfitt, Rhymney Bridge
315	A128 MBA	NIW 6515	Leyland Tiger TRCTL11/3R	Plaxton C49FT	1984	1991	1995	Wimco, Mitcham
316	A133 MBA	NIW 6516	Leyland Tiger TRCTL11/3R	Plaxton C49FT	1984	1991	1995	Dance & Evans, London
317	D537 MVR	NIW 6517	Volvo B10M-61	Van Hool C49FT	1987	1991	1999	Shearings 537
318	C532 DND	NIW 6518	Volvo B10M-61	Van Hool C53F	1986	1991	1996	Shearings 532
392	D87 EDH	NSU 181	MCW Metrorider MF150/9	MCW DP25F	1987	1992	1997	Patrick Collection, Birmingham
382	AAL 468A	LIB 1180	Leyland Leopard PSU5D/4R	Plaxton C53F (1988)	1980	1993	2001	Border Tours, Burnley
319	E329 OMG	NIW 6519	Volvo B10M-61	Van Hool C51FT	1988	1993	1999	Rothwell, Heywood
320	F763 ENE	RJI 8720	Volvo B10M-61	Van Hool C55F	1989	1993	2002	Shearings 763
321	F348 JSU	RJI 8721	Volvo B10M-60	Van Hool C55F	1989	1993	1999	Bruce Coaches, Overtown
322	D709 NYG	RJI 8722	Volvo B10M-61	Van Hool C53F	1987	1993	2002	Clarkson, South Elmsall
393	B183 FDM		Volvo B10M-50	East Lancs CH45/33F	1985	1993	1997	Wright, Wrexham
301	C396 DML	OIW 5801	Leyland Tiger TRCTL11/3RZ	Van Hool C49FT	1985	1994	1998	Lodge, High Easter

No	Reg	Prev reg	Chassis	Body	New	Acquired	Out	Operator / Notes
323	F887 SMU		Volvo B10M-61	Van Hool C49FT	1989	1994	2002	Limebourne, London
324	G94 VFP	RJI 8723	Volvo B10M-60	Van Hool C49FT	1989	1995	1998	Houghton, Woolton
300	N300 EST		Dennis Javelin	Plaxton C48FT	1996		2002	new
333	N585 AWJ	N333 EST	Dennis Javelin	Neoplan C50FT	1996		2001	new
310	A10 TBT		DAF MB230	Van Hool C51F	1989	1996	1997	Venning, Skipton
374	N374 EAK		Volvo B10M-62	Plaxton C49FT	1996	1996	1996	Gardiner, East Kilbride
382	VOY 182X		Leyland Tiger TRCTL11/2R	Plaxton C53F	1981	1996	2001	Border Tours, Burnley
326	M26 HNY		Volvo B12 (T)	Jonkheere C49FT	1994	1996	1999	Bebb, Llantwit Fardre
327	M27 HNY		Volvo B12 (T)	Jonkheere C49FT	1994	1996	1999	Bebb, Llantwit Fardre
	H462 BEU		Volvo B10M-60	Plaxton C51FT	1990	1997	1997	Wessex Coaches, Bristol
	R570 ANB		Volkswagen Caravelle	Volkswagen M7	1997		1999	new
	R343 HCW		Ford Galaxy	Ford M6	1997		1999	new
347	M347 MCY		Dennis Javelin	Berkhof C50FT	1994	1998	MBO	D Coaches, Morriston
348	M348 MCY		Dennis Javelin	Berkhof C50FT	1994	1998	MBO	D Coaches, Morriston
231	T231 JNC		Volkswagen Caravelle	Volkswagen M8	1999		MBO	new
232	T232 JNC		Volkswagen Caravelle	Volkswagen M8	1999		MBO	new
341	T341 NBV		Bova Futura FHD12-340	Bova C49FT	1999		2002	new
342	T342 NBV		Bova Futura FHD12-340	Bova C49FT	1999		2002	new
343	T343 NBV		Bova Futura FHD12-340	Bova C49FT	1999		2002	new
344	T344 NBV		Bova Futura FHD12-340	Bova C49FT	1999		MBO	new
312	NXI 812		Volvo B10M-50	Van Hool C50FT	1989	2000	2000	Viscount Central, Burnley 12
313	GXI 613		Volvo B10M-53	Plaxton CH53/12CT	1989	1999	1999	Viscount Central, Burnley 13
67	G727 JC		Volvo B10M-55	Plaxton DP53F	1989	1999	2002	Goodwin, Eccles
66	G728 JC		Volvo B10M-55	Plaxton DP53F	1989	1999	2002	Goodwin, Eccles
345	W445 CFR		Bova Futura FHD12-370	Bova C49FT	2000		2002	new
346	W446 CFR		Bova Futura FHD12-370	Bova C49FT	2000		2002	new
219	G914 UPP		Mercedes-Benz 709D	Reeve-Burgess B25F	1989	2000	2001	Harrogate & District 219
215	G915 UPP		Mercedes-Benz 709D	Reeve-Burgess B23F	1989	2000	2001	Harrogate & District 216
311	P211 RWR		DAF DE33WSSB3000	Ikarus C51FT	1997		MBO	London Coaches, Northfleet
352	R252 KWY		Bova Futura FHD12-340	Bova C49FT	1998		MBO	Associated, Harlow

Previous registration(s) prior to joining the fleet

66 (G728 JJC) – WSV 550, G900 MNS   67 (G727 JJC) – WSV 553, G899 MNS   310 (A10 TBT) – F270 RJX   312 (NXI 812) – G827 UMU
313 (GXI 613) – F705 COA   322 (D709 NYG) – MIW 2422, D561 MVR   382 (AAL 468A) – BUH 225V

NEW COMPANY FOLLOWING MANAGEMENT BUYOUT FROM ROSSENDALE IN 2002

Reg No	Chassis type	Body type and seating		In	Out	Notes
M347 MCY	Dennis Javelin	Berkhof	C50FT	2002	2003	Ex Rossendale
M348 MCY	Dennis Javelin	Berkhof	C50FT	2002	2004	Ex Rossendale
T231 JNC	VW Caravelle	VW 8		2002		Ex Rossendale
T232 JNC	VW Caravelle	VW 8		2002		Ex Rossendale
T344 NBV	Bova FHD12	Bova	C49FT	2002	2007	Ex Rossendale
P211 RWR	DAF DE33	Ikarus	C51FT	2002	2007	Ex Rossendale
R252 KWY	Bova FHD12	Bova	C49FT	2002	2005	Ex Rossendale
W885 BNA	Iveco 391E	Beulas	C49FT	2003	2006	Ex Jones, Walkden
FG03 JDU	Iveco 391E	Beulas	C49FT	2003		
BX54 EBA	Mercedes Benz Touro	M-B	C49FT	2004		
YJ55 EYV	Bova FHD12	Bova	C53FT	2005		
YJ57 EYS	Bova FHD12	Bova	C49FT	2007		

Eric Smith's decision to retain CDK 448C in 1991, recognising its fine body condition after the refurbishment in 1984, has enabled many older enthusiasts to recapture the glorious days of Harrington-bodied Leyland coaches, not just in the white-liveried Ellen Smith fleet but with other top-line operators. These four views by John Senior show it (above and on the facing page) at a Heart of the Pennines Rally in May 1996, based on the Piece Hall, Halifax, and (below) at the Leyland Celebratory Centenary Event at the National Tramway Museum at Crich in spring 2008. Trips to and from the Stone Chair public house to sample the delights of riding in the vehicles and enjoying the home-cooked food were not to be missed, whilst at Crich the coach was a fine ambassador for Leyland, Harrington and Ellen Smith. *(JAS)*

Though the rear design lost much of its special appeal when Harrington dropped the famous dorsal-fin, the distinctive signwriting still makes CDK 448C instantly recognisable when it fulfils its various rally commitments. *(JAS)*

SDK 442, on the left of the trio of coaches in the upper view, was a Leyland Royal Tiger Worldmaster carrying a Plaxton Consort II centre-door body with seats for 41. In 1970 it received a new Plaxton Panorama Elite body and remained in service in this form (as in the lower picture) until being withdrawn in 1983. SDK 442 was later preserved and as mentioned earlier now resides in the Greater Manchester Transport Society Museum in Boyle Street, Manchester. (*EOC both*)

Upper.:LFS 487T, a 1979 Plaxton-bodied Leopard was numbered 308 by Rossendale and re-registered OIB 3608. It is pictured at the Whit Friday Brass Band Contest at Lydgate in June 1995, carrying the Rossendale scout band. *(EO)*

Lower. FJA 400Y was numbered 305 by Rossendale and remained in the fleet until 1999. It is seen here at Fleetwood in July 1998 on service X79 to the Fylde Coast, sfter being re-registered OIB 6205 *(EO)*

Opposite page: 1983 Plaxton-bodied Tiger FJA 400Y stands in Ypres Market Place in Belgium on a tour of First World War battlefields driven by Jack Mills. The magnificent Cloth Hall, almost razed to the ground, was rebuilt after the war. *(DNC)*

The rear view, (upper photo), taken on the garage forecourt, shows the familiar ribbon logo on the boot door. *(JJH)*

The lower photograph shows similar B887 WRJ parked at Manchester University. Rossendale later re-registered it OIB 5403. *(DN)*

Leyland Doyen D387 VAO, the former demonstrator, was built at the Leyland factory near Workington, hence the Carlisle registration. It joined the fleet the following year retaining its demonstration livery throughout its life with the family company as shown in the upper picture with Alan Schofield at the wheel. In 1991 Rossendale repainted it, numbered it 302 and re-registered it OIB 5402. In the lower photograph it stands, freshly painted, in Rossendale's Rochdale yard. *(EO; JJH)*

Opposite page: LIB 1184, originally NDW 148X, new in 1982, was a former Rossendale vehicle that arrived in 1986 from Hill's of Tredegar. In 1994 it was transferred to the Ellen Smith fleet and repainted into the revised fleet livery, for use on the express services from Oldham, Rochdale and East Lancashire to the Fylde Coast as lettered on the side when seen in Fleetwood. *(MB via HP)*

A new chassis/body combination for the fleet, M347 MCY was a 1994 Dennis Javelin with Berkhof 50-seat body. It was one of a pair acquired from D Coaches of Morriston, near Swansea, in 1998 and formed part of the new Ellen Smith Company's fleet in 2002. It is seen here at the Folkestone terminal of Le Shuttle on a David Urquhart holiday tour in June 2000, still bearing the Elite Tours logo as well as the redesigned leaping tiger. *(EO)*

B183 FDM (opposite page) was a 1985 Volvo B10M with East Lancashire Coachbuilders 78 seat bodywork and was the first double-decker to wear Ellen Smith livery. What would Harry and Eric have thought? The vehicle was purchased from Wright of Wrexham in 1993 and was extensively refurbished, including the fitting of new coach seats, prior to it entering service in the Spring of 1994, as number 393. In this guise, it ran for just over 3 years before transferring to the Rossendale fleet where it remained until 2000 and then was sold to local operator Pioneer of Rochdale, who occupied part of the Corporation Road yard site. It was re-registered 479 DKH with its new owner and now resides in Scotland with Liddell, Auchinleck. It was still in use in April 2010, now in its 25th year of service.*(EO)*

Opposite page: Acquired in 1999 from Viscount Central of Burnley, NXI 812, formerly G827 UMU, a ten year-old Volvo B10M with Van Hool 50-seat body had a relatively short stay in the fleet and was sold the following year to Haydock (East Lancashire Coaches) of Oswaldtwistle. It is seen here at Manchester University in June 1999. *(EO)*

As related in the text, Paul Targett and John White of Rossendale Transport took over the Ellen Smith subsidiary in a management buy-out in 2002. The initial fleet was gradually withdrawn and new vehicles bought. The livery was changed to a striking overall black and a new tiger's head and logo introduced. *(NO)*

The first new coach was FG03 JDU, an Iveco 391E with Beulas 49-seat body, photographed in the Rochdale yard in December 2007. *(NO)*

Pictured in Skipton in February 2009 is BX54 EBA, a Mercedes-Benz Touro dating from 2004. *(NO)*

YJ55 EYV, a Bova FHD12 new in 2005, is seen on a day excursion to Fleetwood and Freeport in March 2009. *(NO)*

YJ57 EYS, a Bova FHD12, is caught between tours in the yard at Rochdale in May 2009. *(JJH)*